MULTIPLE PERSONALITY DISORDER,

PSYCHOLOGICAL OR DEMONIC?

BY
PHILLIP SPENCER MORRIS, Ph.D.
HIGHLANDS, TEXAS
U.S.A.

Copyright © 2008 by Dr. Phillip S. Morris

Multiple Personality Disorder, Psychological or Demonic?
by Dr. Phillip S. Morris

Printed in the United States of America

ISBN 9781606477328

All rights reserved solely by the author. The author guarantees all contents are original and do not infringe upon the legal rights of any other person or work. No part of this book may be reproduced in any form without the permission of the author. The views expressed in this book are not necessarily those of the publisher.

Unless otherwise indicated, Bible quotations are taken from The New King James Version. Copyright © 1982 by Thomas Nelson, Inc.

www.xulonpress.com

TABLE OF CONTENTS

Illustrations	vii
Acknowledgments	ix
Endorsements	xi
Preface	xiii
Introduction	xvii
What Is A Personality?	21
Double-Minded	35
The Importance of a Name	42
Multiple Personality Disorder and "Alter Personalities"	54
The Three-Fold being of Man	59
Biblical Case of Multiple Personality: Demoniac – Multiple	70
Dissociation	78
Dissociation and Amnesia	103
Unequally Yoked With Unbelievers	114
Support Systems	130
Integration	142
Treatment Modalities	153

Emotional Inner Healing 185
Conclusion 199
Bibliography 201
About The Author 205

ILLUSTRATIONS

FIGURES

1. Old Testament Temple 60
2. Clinical Expression Of Dissociation 66
3. Emotions Gradation Scale 80
4. Abrupt Change In Emotions Causing Dissociation 81
5. Point Of Spirit's Entry 82
6. Personality Map 87
7. Clinical Expression Of Dissociation 104
8. Demonic Personality Layout..123
9. Life's Information In Memories..134

ACKNOWLEDGMENTS

First of all, I want to thank my Lord and Savior Jesus Christ who called me into His family and entrusted me with helping mend broken people.

My wife, Maribel, has graciously put up with me during this prolonged journey of much starting and stopping in this endeavor. If anyone has written a dissertation, you know what I mean. Thank you, sweetheart.

I also want to thank my spiritual daughter, Sheri Hoffee, who has prayed for me and helped with the editing of this paper.

Karen Jackson helped on my master's thesis and was a reader on this project as well. Thanks again, Karen.

I want to thank Bridgett Porter for her help in typing some of the manuscript.

Thanks to Virginia Schramek who, as a professional proofreader, really located all my errors.

But none of this would have been possible if hurting people would not have trusted me to help them. They are the ones who worked so hard and deserve the most recognition and applause for their brave journey to freedom.

ENDORSEMENTS

I highly recommend this book to deliverance ministers. The problem of multiple personalities surfaces in ministry quite often and it is so good to learn from Dr. Phillip Morris, who has been a successful practitioner with years of experience. I especially enjoyed the solid Scriptural backing all through this work. This is a must for every deliverance minister's library, in my opinion.

Doris M. Wagner; Co-Founder, International Society of Deliverance Ministers

From first hand observation, I have witnessed Dr. Phillip Morris used mightily by God to set the captives free. This book demystifies difficult unchartered waters that the Body of Christ simply cannot remain naive about. Sophisticated demonic structures are an unfortunate reality that must be eradicated in the earth today. Reading this book will thrust you from a ground level to a graduate level understanding of deliverance in an effort to fulfill one of our fundamental God ordained mandates from the Lord Jesus Christ: To set the captives free!

Rev. Jill Mitchell O'Brien, President - Kingdom Connections International, Inc., Houston, TX

This book is a must read for anyone in a deliverance ministry or is interested in the total freedom that God has made available to all of us. My husband and I personally have worked along with Dr. Morris during deliverance sessions and witnessed many Christians being set free from demonic influences; some of which are described in this writing. I personally lived for 10 years with my husband who, before deliverance, was definitely two distinct personalities. With the leading of the Holy Spirit, the Grace of God, and several deliverance sessions with Dr. Morris, my husband is a free man today serving God with a heart after Jesus. Dr. Morris has transferred the wisdom he has, and is practicing, into this book for all of us to learn. When you allow God to bring forth the revelation, this is an eye opening experience.

Pastor Karen Jackson, Our Fellowship Christian Church, Houston, TX

PREFACE

First, I want to give the history that has led me to the beliefs I hold and will state in this book. God thrust me into the deliverance ministry in August of 1982. I was seeing some astounding results; however, the people did not seem to retain their freedom more than three to six months. I told God this was too much work to only achieve that level of results. If it was not going to last any longer than that, I was not going to do this anymore. In the mid 1980's I was the pastor of a church, but I refused to work in deliverance. I told the people we were going to have a "balanced" church. Evidently, it is hard to be "balanced" without the freedom that comes from deliverance ministry. That pastorate lasted for only two and a half years. During a revival meeting, God spoke to me and said, ***"Close the church and go back to school to finish your education."*** I had been in rebellion to God by not working in deliverance ministry. God wanted me to learn how to help people obtain, retain, and maintain their freedom. The following Sunday morning I preached a sermon titled ***"The Brook has Dried Up"***; told the people of some good churches in the area to pray about attending, locked the doors, and followed God back to school.

While I was attending Gulf Coast Bible College, the president called me "The Giant Slayer"; and said, "Keep on slaying those giants, Phillip." I believe the strongholds in people are giants that must be dealt with in the spiritual, as well as emotional and mental realms. Thus, my Master's thesis is titled **"Spiritual Connections to Personality Disorders"**. I believe the spiritual connections that interfere with a person's ability to think and act correctly are demonic.

I re-enrolled in Bible College; finished my undergraduate degree in Psychology, and went on to earn my Master's Degree in Pastoral Counseling from Houston Graduate School of Theology. I did all the course work to be licensed by the state of Texas as a "Licensed Professional Counselor". However, because of the restrictions of the state requirements, I felt God did not want the state of Texas involved in His ministry, so I did not get my license. I believe that I had to have the degrees for the credibility to be able to reach into, not necessarily secular psychiatry, but the Christian side of the psychiatric industry.

During the time I was working on my undergraduate and Masters degree in counseling and psychology, I believe God protected my mind from becoming caught up in psychiatric knowledge by thrusting me into the deliverance ministry. Psychiatry teaches someone how to cope with problems; but through the Lord's deliverance, one can receive freedom from the cause of the problem. Over the years, the Lord has blessed us with the opportunity to work with people who have had what psychiatrists would diagnose as "Multiple Personality Disorder" or "MPD". In this book, I want to share with you my theories concerning MPD, as well as some clients' histories, problems, and treatment methods we used to bring about real freedom in their lives.

I have omitted some names to protect the identity of the brave people who have been set free.

INTRODUCTION

Since I began doing this in 1982, some of the people I have worked with presented with distinct multiple personalities. I do not agree with the secular diagnosis, or the prescribed treatment of "Multiple Personality Disorder", but I am using the terminology because more people are familiar with it. According to the Diagnostic and Statistical Manual of Mental Disorders, Third Edition Revised, a person with MPD may have "two or more fully developed personalities or one distinct personality with one or more personality states". Also, "the belief that one is possessed by another person, spirit, or entity may occur as a symptom of MPD. In such cases the complaint of being "possessed" is actually the experience of the alternate personality's influence on the person's behavior and mood."

The different personalities usually are formed during dissociation episodes from traumatic events in a person's life. My experience has shown that the "personalities" that are formed, are in reality nests of demons manifesting as personalities. When a demon invades and influences a person's life, it will manifest traits that appear as human characteristics, but it is not the real person's true personality. I make no apologies for the fact that I only work with born again Christians. Jesus taught that deliverance was the children's bread and only for those who believe in Him.

> **And behold, <u>a woman of Canaan</u> came from that region and cried out to Him, saying, "Have mercy on me, O Lord, Son of David! My daughter is severely demon-possessed." ²³ But He answered her not a word. And His disciples came and urged Him, saying, "Send her away, for she cries out after us." ²⁴ But He answered and said, "<u>I was not sent except to the lost sheep of the house of Israel.</u>" ²⁵ Then she came and worshiped Him, saying, "Lord, help me!" ²⁶ But He answered and said, <u>"It is not good to take the children's bread and throw *it* to the little dogs."</u> ²⁷ And she said, "Yes, <u>Lord</u>, yet even the little dogs eat the crumbs which fall from their <u>masters'</u> table." ²⁸ Then Jesus answered and said to her, "O woman, great *is* your faith! Let it be to you as you desire." And her daughter was healed from that very hour.**
>
> **Matthew 15:22-28**

When this Gentile woman came to Jesus for her daughter's deliverance, He did nothing until she identified Jesus as her Lord and Master.

I believe this problem is spiritual in nature and must be addressed spiritually. Therefore, faith in Jesus Christ as Lord and belief in His delivering and healing powers are imperative. I will defuse the fear of the belief that a born again Christian may be "possessed"; they are "oppressed" - not possessed. I intend to show that when a spirit gains entrance to one's soul, it becomes the "strongman" and everything that develops after that is not of God, but demonic. And finally, I will relate experiences of deliverance and restoration through the treatment methods used in this ministry.

WHAT IS A PERSONALITY?

Carl Jung, Katharine C. Briggs, and Isabel Briggs Myers have researched and developed several different personality types. Carl Jung believed that there were two basic kinds of "functions" which humans used in their lives: how we take in information ("perceive" things) and how we make decisions. He believed that within these two categories, there were two opposite ways of functioning. We can perceive information via 1) our senses or 2) our intuition. We can make decisions based on 1) objective logic or 2) subjective feelings. Jung believed that we all use these four functions in our lives, but that each individual uses the different functions with a varying amount of success and frequency. He believed that we could identify an order of preference for these functions within individuals. The function which someone uses most frequently is their "dominant" function. The dominant function is supported by an auxiliary (2nd) function, tertiary (3rd) function, and inferior (4th) function. He asserted that individuals either "extraverted" or "introverted" their dominant function. He felt that the dominant function was so important that it overshadowed all of the other functions in terms of defining personality type. Therefore, Jung defined eight personality types:

1. Extraverted Sensing (modern types: ESFP, ESTP)
2. Introverted Sensing (modern types: ISTJ, ISFJ)
3. Extraverted Intuition (modern types: ENFP, ENTP)
4. Introverted Intuition (modern types: INFJ, INTJ)
5. Extraverted Thinking (modern types: ESTJ, ENTJ)
6. Introverted Thinking (modern types: ISTP, INTP)
7. Extraverted Feeling (modern types: ESFJ, ENFJ)
8. Introverted Feeling (modern types: INFP, ISFP)

Internet article

Jung also taught that:

"introverts focus on their inner world of thoughts, intuitions, emotions, and sensations; extroverts are more oriented toward the outer world, other people, and material goods. Each person has a mixture of both components. The persona is the mask covering the personality that the person presents to the outside world. The persona may become fixed so that the real person is hidden from himself or herself." **(1)**

Another popular personality classification system has four "types":

- The **Sanguine** is the **popular person** who wants to have fun out of every situation and be the life of the party. Sanguines love to talk.
- The **Choleric** is the **powerful person** who wants to take control of every situation and make decisions for others. Cholerics love to work.
- The **Melancholy** is the **perfect person** who wants everything done in order and done properly and who appreciates art and music. Melancholies love to analyze.
- The **Phlegmatic** is the **peaceful person** who wants to stay out of trouble, keep life on an even keel, and get along with everybody. Phlegmatics like to rest.

There are some personality tests that include as many as sixteen different personalities. It can be very confusing, especially when the ones who developed the "types" will state that no one is just one type, but will fluctuate between more than one and possibly will operate in all of them!

Let us look at two well-respected definitions of a personality:

"Personality traits are enduring patterns of perceiving, relating to, and thinking about the environment and one

self, and are exhibited in a wide range of important social and personal contexts." (2)

Personality: 3. *Psychol. "All the constitutional, mental, emotional, social, etc. characteristics of an individual. An organized pattern of all the characteristics of an individual." (3)*

That is a clinical way to say, "*It is how you present yourself and the impression you make on others.*" Have you ever known anybody that one day is one way, and the next day another? Or changes within the hour, or quicker? We usually say, "*That's his personality. That's just the way he is.*" Actually, what you are saying is: "*That's the way he presents himself.*"

I want us to look at some people in the Bible that presented themselves one way and then another at certain times. It seems like they were having trouble figuring out what "type" of personality they were.

> **'if the <u>spirit of jealousy</u> comes upon him and he becomes jealous of his wife, who has defiled herself; or if the <u>spirit of jealousy</u> comes upon him and he becomes jealous of his wife, although she has not defiled herself—**
>
> **Numbers 5:14**

This man became so jealous he took his wife to the priest to evoke a curse upon her whether she was unfaithful or not. He was being controlled by something different than his normal behavior.

> **My people ask counsel from their wooden idols, and their staff informs them. For the <u>spirit of harlotry</u> has caused them to stray, and they have played the harlot against their God.   Hosea 4:12**

> **My people ask counsel at their stocks, and their staff declareth unto them: for the <u>spirit of whoredoms</u> hath caused them to err, and they have gone a whoring from under their God.   Hosea 4:12 (KJV)**

In this verse, when people gave a spirit authority in their lives by worshipping other gods, that spirit overpowered their normal judgment and they were led astray. In the New King James Version it was called a spirit of <u>harlotry</u>, but <u>whoredoms</u> was used in the King James Version.

> **And behold, there was a woman who had a <u>spirit of infirmity</u> eighteen years, and was bent over and could in no way raise herself up.   Luke 13:11**

This woman would have been "classified" as a cripple because she had been in this shape for eighteen years. But Jesus knew it was only a spirit that caused this condition, and when He laid his hands on her the spirit left, and she immediately straightened up. She was no longer "classified" a cripple, but now she "presented" herself as a different person.

> **Now it happened, as we went to prayer, that a certain slave girl possessed with a <u>spirit of divination</u> met us, who brought her masters much profit by fortune-telling.**
> **Acts 16:16**

This slave girl could either operate in fortunetelling or her normal personality depending on the spirit within her. This is evident when Paul cast out the spirit and she could no longer bring her masters much profit and they became outraged and started a riot in the town against Paul and the others.

> **What do you want? Shall I come to you with a rod, or in love and a <u>spirit of gentleness</u>?   1 Corinthians 4:21**

> **Brethren, if a man is overtaken in any trespass, you who are spiritual restore such a one in a <u>spirit of gentleness</u>, considering yourself lest you also be tempted.**
> **Galatians 6:1**

These two verses seem to suggest one can present oneself as a gentle or a rougher personality.

For you did not receive the <u>spirit of bondage again to fear</u>, but you received the Spirit of adoption by whom we cry out, "Abba, Father." Romans 8:15

For God has not given us a <u>spirit of fear</u>, but (a <u>spirit</u>) of <u>power</u> and <u>of love</u> and <u>of a sound mind.</u> 2 Timothy 1:7

We are of God. He who knows God hears us; he who is not of God does not hear us. By this we know the <u>spirit of truth</u> and the <u>spirit of error</u>. 1 John 4:6

In these verses we see when one is controlled by a demonic spirit, it will change the way he presents himself. A spirit of fear causes one to present as introverted and shy, or a person can present himself as one in control operating in love and a sound mind. In the second verse, we see that a spirit can interfere with a person's ability to discern truth or error. With the spirit of error, one cannot hear or understand the Word of God, but with the spirit of truth one will be able to present oneself as a hearing and obedient servant of God.

Through these verses we see that demonic spirits can influence our behaviors and the image we portray. Thanks be to God, we are not at the mercy of the demonic spiritual realm, but God has provided for us everything we need to rule and reign in this life.

> **Grace and peace be multiplied to you in the knowledge of God and of Jesus our Lord, ³as <u>His divine power has given to us all things that _pertain_ to life and godliness</u>, through the knowledge of Him who called us by glory and virtue, ⁴by which have been <u>given to us exceedingly great and precious promises</u>, that through these <u>you may be partakers of the divine nature</u>, having <u>escaped the corruption _that is_ in the world through lust</u>.**
>
> **2 Peter 1:2-4**

God has given Christians everything that pertains to life and godliness, which affords us the ability to operate in a spirit of a sound mind. And through the great and precious promises of God, we may be partakers of the divine nature and escape the corruption that is in the world. In other words, we do not have to be ruled by "types" of personalities, but we have an example and "type" to which we are to attain. That "type" is the model that Jesus portrayed while He walked on this earth. Jesus demonstrated different characteristic traits depending upon the situation. But He always allowed Holy Spirit to lead and dictate at the moment. He described this as doing and saying what His Father did, thus, always pleasing the Father. Jesus said this is how we will be when we are born of the Spirit.

Do not marvel that I said to you, 'You must be born again.' ⁸The wind blows where it wishes, and you hear the sound of it, but cannot tell where it comes from and where it goes. <u>So is everyone who is born of the Spirit</u>."

John 3:7-8

They did not understand that He spoke to them of the Father. ²⁸Then Jesus said to them, "When you lift up the Son of Man, then you will know that I am *He,* and *that* I do nothing of Myself; but <u>as My Father taught Me, I speak these things</u>. ²⁹And He who sent Me is with Me. The Father has not left Me alone, for <u>I always do those things that please Him</u>." **John 8:27-29**

For I have not spoken on My own *authority;* but <u>the Father who sent Me gave Me a command, what I should say and what I should speak</u>. ⁵⁰And I know that His command is everlasting life. Therefore, <u>whatever I speak, just as the Father has told Me, so I speak</u>." **John 12:49-50**

During the death of Jesus' good friend Lazarus, Jesus gave us a demonstration of being led by the Holy Spirit. He was not dictated by a "type" of personality or driven by emotions to do anything, but instead prayed, listened, and waited for the clear leading of Holy

Spirit, who is the light of this world. This is our model of the "type" of personality to attain.

> **So, when He heard that he (Lazarus) was sick, <u>He stayed two more days</u> in the place where He was. ⁷Then after this He said to *the* disciples, "Let us go to Judea again." ⁸*The* disciples said to Him, "Rabbi, lately the Jews sought to stone You, and are You going there again?" ⁹Jesus answered, "Are there not twelve hours in the day? <u>If anyone walks in the day, he does not stumble, because he sees the light of this world.</u> ¹⁰But if one walks in the night, he stumbles, because the light is not in him."**
>
> **John 11:6-10**

In the darkest moment of Jesus' life on earth, in the Garden of Gethsemane before His betrayal, He would not be dictated by a "type" or classification of personality; instead, He yielded His will to that of His Father in heaven.

> **saying, "Father, if it is Your will, take this cup away from Me; <u>nevertheless not My will, but Yours, be done</u>."**
>
> **Luke 22:42**

Paul said that we have the mind of Christ and we are to be perfect even as our Father in heaven is perfect. We need to look at

God's creation from God's perspective, in a spiritual manner, to understand how we are to operate.

> **Now we have received, not the spirit of the world, but the Spirit who is from God, that we might know the things that have been freely given to us by God. ¹³These things we also speak, not in words which man's wisdom teaches but which the Holy Spirit teaches, <u>comparing spiritual things with spiritual</u>. ¹⁴But the natural man does not receive the things of the Spirit of God, for they are foolishness to him; nor can he know *them*, because they are spiritually discerned. ¹⁵But he who is spiritual judges all things, yet he himself is *rightly* judged by no one. ¹⁶For *"who has known the mind of the LORD that he may instruct Him?"* But <u>we have the mind of Christ</u>.**
>
> 1 Corinthians 2:12-16

> **Therefore <u>you shall be perfect</u>, just as your Father in heaven is perfect.**   **Matthew 5:48**

The Greek word translated "perfect" in this scripture is teleios; and means that we are to be **complete** in our mental and moral character.

teleios, Greek 5046, Strong's: <u>*complete*</u> (in various applications of labor, growth, <u>mental and moral character</u>, etc.); (4)

To be complete, I believe, is to operate as God intended with a sound mind and one personality – a loving and caring person who is operating in spiritual authority with the help of the indwelling Spirit of God. Jesus gave us the commands we are to follow and the Spirit to accomplish them. He also said we are to be one in Spirit and mind, even as He and Father God are one. If Jesus has commanded and prayed for us to do this, it must be possible. God is not the author of confusion, but of peace.

> **"Teacher, which *is* the great commandment in the law?" 37Jesus said to him, *"'You shall <u>love the L<small>ORD</small> your God with all your heart, with all your soul, and with all your mind.'</u> 38This is the* first and great commandment. 39And *the* second *is* like it: 'You shall <u>love your neighbor as yourself.</u>' 40On these two commandments hang all the Law and the Prophets."   Matthew 22:36-40**

> **"I do not pray for these alone, but also for those who will believe in Me through their word; 21that <u>they all may be one, as You, Father, *are* in Me, and I in You; that they also may be one in Us</u>, that the world may believe that**

You sent Me. ²²And the glory which You gave Me I have given them, that <u>they may be one just as We are one</u>:

John 17:20-22

For <u>God is not *the author* of confusion but of peace</u>, as in all the churches of the saints.

1 Corinthians 14:33

Secular psychiatry can be very confusing, but in the next chapter I will show how a person with demon influenced "double-mind" can really be confused and not be able to receive from God.

NOTES: WHAT IS A PERSONALITY?

1 Kaplan, Harold I., and Benjamin J. Sadock. Synopsis of Psychiatry: Behavioral Sciences, Clinical Psychiatry, 5th ed. (Baltimore: Williams & Wilkins, 1988), 148.

2 The American Psychiatric Association: Diagnostic and Statistical Manual of Mental Disorders, 3rd ed. (Washington, DC: American Psychiatric Association, 1987), 335.

3 Barnhart, C. L. & Jess Stein, eds, American College Dictionary, (New York: Random House, 1967), 904

4 James Strong, Strong's Exhaustive Concordance: Compact Edition, (Grand Rapids: Baker Book House, 1982), 784

DOUBLE-MINDED

God likes for preachers to practice what they preach. Early in our ministry, when we were working with people we were not aware of their problems. But then God would give me revelation knowledge, and we would be able to recognize the symptoms. As He would give us more understanding on a particular problem, more and more people with that problem would come to our office. With each new revelation He gave us, we would have an opportunity to walk it out. One particular situation was about the difficulties experienced by a "double-minded" man. One day I received a revelation on **James 1:6-8**:

> **"But let him ask in faith, with no doubting, for he who doubts is like a wave of the sea driven and tossed by the wind. For let not that man suppose that he will receive anything from the Lord; he is a <u>double-minded</u> man, unstable in all his ways."**

The word "double-minded" is "dipsuchos" in Greek, which means "two-souled":

dipsuchos, Greek 1374, Strong's; from Greek 1364 (dis) and Greek 5590 (psuche); *two-spirited*, **i.e.** *vacillating* **(in opinion or purpose): double minded. (5)**

Dipsuchos comes from two words "dis" and "psuche". Psuche is our soul – mind, will, and emotions. God created us with only one soul, not two or more. If there is more than one, it is there illegally. An "illegal soul" will cause a person to be in confusion and unsure of what he really needs or wants, or even who he really is. This will give the appearance of more than one personality in the person. God called this "unstable" in all he does, and that is not the way God created us.

One night while in a meeting with two of the Freedom Fighters ministry directors, a lady called my office and asked, *"Can you do something about our daughter? She is 18 months old and just screams and screams and won't stop. I don't know what is going on; but I am concerned about this and I need some help. I think there is something in this house, or something."* We went over to her house right then. Her baby had been screaming like this for almost two weeks now. They could not sleep, and the household was a mess. The parents were trying to go to work during the day and then could not sleep at night. They took the baby to the doctor, and he pre-

Multiple Personality Disorder, Psychological or Demonic?

scribed medicines after medicines. None of the medicines worked, and the baby would not sleep. He even was contemplating giving sedatives to an 18-month old baby! Another strange thing about this baby was the fact that she had never spoken any words. Eighteen months old and had never even said Mama or Dada.

We went to their home and began praying through the house to spiritually clean the house. This family knew about deliverance and spiritual warfare, so we only found a few things that would draw spirits and told them, *"If this was our house, we would get rid of these things."* We do not personally throw away other people's things. They removed them from the house, and we began to deal specifically with the baby.

This little, 18 month old baby would rear up and scream hysterically; sometimes it was even a growl that came out of her. We were trying to hold her and keep her on the couch. She was wrestling back and forth on the couch and wearing out two adult men! We were just trying to keep her on the couch! There were all kinds of things going on spiritually. Finally, at my wit's end, I said, *"God, I have no idea what is going on here, but I know that your Word says we wrestle not against flesh and blood. This is wearing me out, and I am going to stop. I am not going to wrestle this baby any more. I'm not going to do another thing until You tell me something."*

I had bound and cast out everything I knew. I came against every principality in the air and everything on the earth, above, under, and in! I did everything I knew to do and anything that I even thought might help. But all to no avail. I didn't know what else to do, so I went over and sat down in a rocking chair; just relaxed, rocked and prayed in tongues. About five minutes later the mother said, *"By the way, our baby has been adopted, and I know the name the agency gave her. Do you think that would make any difference?"* I said, *"I don't know, but we'll try it."* The baby had been born three months prematurely in the month of April so the agency named her April. Three months later, this family adopted her and changed her name to E_____.

By this time, Dad had picked the baby up and was trying to contain her. Dad is about 6'2", and she was climbing all over him like a jungle-gym. She was wearing him out and wouldn't stop screaming. I was still sitting in the chair and I said, *"In the name of Jesus, I bind that spirit, that illegal soul of April, and I break your hold and command you to leave her right now in Jesus' name."* **Immediately**, she yawned twice, laid her head on Dad's shoulder and went sound asleep. I thought Dad was going to have a heart attack. She had total peace and was sleeping soundly. E_____ slept all night, and they had to wake her up the next morning. She has not had any trouble since then.

We also commanded the spirit of death to leave E_____ and the house. Death had tried to claim E_____ in the womb – three months premature birth – and was now trying again. We also prayed for dad and mom and the other two children that night. They all received great freedom through deliverance and slept very well that night.

When the other kids were awakened in the morning, they sniffed the air and said, "The house smells different". Hallelujah! The presence of God will make a difference in everything.

After that night, I was thinking, *"WHOA! What do we have here?"* I still didn't know what was going on. Then the Lord revealed to me that this was an illegal soul that had gained entrance at birth. Without legal parents to assume responsibility and name her, she was labeled "April" and an "illegal soul" entered. I use the term "illegal soul" but it is a spirit. This is an example of "dipsuchos" - "two-souled" found in the scriptures in James:

> **If any of you lacks wisdom, let him ask of God, who gives to all liberally and without reproach, and it will be given to him. 6But let him ask in faith, with no doubting, for he who doubts is like a wave of the sea driven and tossed by the wind. 7For let not that man suppose that he will receive anything from the Lord; 8***he is* **a <u>double-minded man, unstable in all his ways</u>.**   **James 1:5-8**

That spirit, or "illegal soul" called "April", was fighting for the control of this baby's body, and I had to deal with it in the spiritual realm. I bound it and commanded it to leave (cast it out) just as Jesus did in the Bible. When I did, E_____ finally had peace and could go to sleep. I have wondered if God designed for me to begin with a baby; so I could not talk to her and try to figure this out with my finite mind. I give God the glory for everything I know; it is His ministry.

One lady came to our deliverance meeting who was being treated by a psychiatrist from University of Texas Mental Sciences Institute. She had been diagnosed as having atypical Bipolar Disorder and a Borderline Personality Disorder by Dr. Phillip L. and was receiving both medications and individual psychotherapy. Later during our sessions, she related to me times in her life when she would wake up in the morning to find clothing and other things in her room that she had obviously worn the night before, but with no knowledge of what happened. This was an obvious case of another personality manifesting. While I was ministering deliverance in the meeting, the demons in her resisted; but when I ministered as the father to his children, she screamed and fell on the floor and was delivered. I told her to continue seeing her psychiatrist until he wrote her a clean bill of health. She continued for another six months and he tried everything he could to "trigger" her into an episode of dissociation, but to no avail. He wrote her a letter that she no longer was Borderline Personality. You can read her complete testimony, and the doctor's letter, in my book, **"Spiritual Connections to Personality Disorder"**. She became our church secretary for the next nine years!

NOTES: DOUBLE MINDED

5 James Strong, *Strong's Exhaustive Concordance: Compact Edition*, (Grand Rapids: Baker Book House, 1982), 278.

THE IMPORTANCE OF A NAME

◧ — ◨

What is your given name at birth - (The first name on your birth certificate)? If you have been adopted and your name has been changed, that can cause you problems. Remember I told you about April and E_____. There was a change of names and it caused problems. In the Bible God changed names, but He did it for a reason. **Jacob** was no longer a **"deceiver"**; but he became **Israel – "he will rule as God"**. **Abram** was no longer **"high father"**; but he became **Abraham** – the **"Father of many nations"**. **Jesus** is the salvation of mankind and His name means - **"He will save His people from their sins." Immanuel** is: **"God with us."** When God named you, there was a reason.

After the baby incident (April and E_____), a man came to me that was called by a certain name. He thought that was his name until he was seventeen years old and went to get his driver's license. He gave the man at the license branch his birth certificate, and when the guy asked him what his name was, he said, *"Walt."* The DPS officer said, "No, it's Howard." He did not believe him; he had to look at the birth certificate.

The cycle of events in Howard/Walt's life is as follows: while he was in his mother's womb, she already had four sons and said, *"I am not going to have another boy. I had better have a girl; I do not want another boy. If I don't have a girl, I don't even want him."* This was tremendous rejection in the mother's womb. When she had a male baby, the family was so afraid of what she would do, that the aunt didn't even tell Mom what she had. The aunt was so afraid to tell Mom who and what he was that the aunt went ahead and named him Howard. When they got home Mom said, *"Where is my baby?"* They brought him in and told her that he was named Howard. She said, *"No, I'll not have a Howard in my house. We'll call him Walt."* So he went through life thinking his name was Walt. He suffered rejection in the womb and was re-named Walt out of mom's rebellion. This caused Walt to be very rebellious toward God, his responsibilities as a husband and a father, and as a businessman. Sometimes he wouldn't get out of bed all day - just totally rebellious.

When Howard was manifesting, God would speak through him and he would prophesy and flow in the gifts of the Spirit. The prophecies would be right on, and there would be healings and miracles; it was awesome! Whenever Howard was out, he was pleasant and would give you anything he had. But whenever Walt came out and began to manifest, he was so contrary I didn't want to be around him. He was selfish, contrary, and mean to people.

The DSM III-R definition says nothing about amnesia, and it is widely accepted that some people who are obviously multiples show no clear-cut signs of amnesia. Granted, amnesia episodes are an almost certain indicator of multiplicity, but when those episodes are not present, <u>MPD still can be detected by a more subtle sign – switching.</u> (6)

This explains what I experienced one day while I was talking to Howard. We were sitting and having a wonderful conversation when all of a sudden he **switched,** and Walt started talking. There was a change in voice, mood, and attitude. I just looked at him and said, "*In the name of Jesus Christ of Nazareth I bind you, and I refuse to talk to Walt. I will not talk to you. Walt, shut up. I will only talk to Howard.*" We just sat there, staring at each other, and a little bit later Howard started talking again. The next day he asked me, "*Why did you choke me last night?*" I said, "*I didn't choke you.*" He said, "*Something grabbed me right by the throat, and I couldn't talk or say a word.*" That is how powerful the authority of the Name of Jesus is; it stopped that demon.

He didn't like the name of Howard, and it took a long time for him to accept that name. But when he was ready to accept it, he was delivered. The biggest problem was all his friends, family, and associates knew him as Walt and kept bringing him back. They would continue to call him Walt, and it would give credence to the wrong

Multiple Personality Disorder, Psychological or Demonic?

spirit. It is very important that everyone support a person who is coming out of a situation like this. It is very important to call them by their given name. By the way, **Howard** is now the pastor of a church in Houston, Texas.

We ministered to a girl from Texas who's given name was Da_____, but she went by Do_____. I ministered deliverance to her, and then I told her, *"I am not going to say that you have to go back to your birth name. But I can tell you what happens. You have the choice. I cannot make you do anything. But you go back to the hotel and pray about it. Come back tomorrow before you go back home."* She came back the next morning and said, *"You know what? I believe God has told me I have to go by Da_____."* I said, *"Praise the Lord."* After her deliverance, she went home and within a week she totally redecorated her apartment. Her apartment was decorated in Southwestern motif with all the Indian stuff that contains a lot of witchcraft designs; and draws evil spirits. She did a spiritual house cleaning and got rid of it all, but it was too much of a shock. Sometimes it is wise to proceed slowly in new territory. I advised her not to redecorate so quickly, but she was excited about her new life and rushed into it. A person needs to be filled with the Word of God and strong enough to resist the enemy, or they will come back. This is spoken of in the Bible in both the Old and New Testament.

I will not drive them out from before you in one year, <u>lest the land become desolate and the beast of the field become</u>

too numerous for you. <u>30</u>Little by little I will drive them out from before you, **until you have increased**, and **you inherit the land.** Exodus 23:29-30

"**When an unclean spirit goes out of a man, he goes through dry places, seeking rest, and finds none. 44Then he says, 'I will return to my house from which I came.' And when he comes, he finds *it* empty, swept, and put in order. 45Then he goes and takes with him seven other spirits more wicked than himself, and they enter and dwell there**; and the last *state* of that man is worse than the first. So shall it also be with this wicked generation."
                                            Matthew 12:43-45

Even when the devil tempted Jesus unsuccessfully, he was looking for another opportunity to return.

Now when the devil had ended every temptation, he departed from Him until an opportune time. Luke 4:13

That nest of demons, Do_____, came back. Do_____ came knocking on the door, Da_____ was not strong enough to resist, and the last I heard she will not even go to church. She refused to come back to see me; and she will not even talk to her friends. She is in a lot of trouble because she chose to go with the demonic. God will not be mocked; the Word is true. It will happen.

Do not be deceived, God is not mocked; for whatever a man sows, that he will also reap.

Galatians 6:7

Usually people will change their name out of rebellion. I don't like my name, so I think I will change it. I'm talking about first names, not last names. Although, one lady came in who had been married three times. She had her maiden name and three last names, and she had been adopted. She had been in foster homes and had even taken some of the foster parent's names because they were kind to her. I had her break all soul-ties with those names. Then I bound them up and said, *"In the name of Jesus, you cannot stay. You must go."* I named each name and commanded it to go. Afterwards, the woman didn't know who she was and got lost going home. It was such a tremendous change to her and she was a little disoriented. She called me, I prayed with her, she found her way home; and this has not happened again. This is not the norm; it has only happened this one time.

A person who is suffering with MPD has believed these lies their whole life. They may believe this is as good as life can be. They will need to be loved and supported and taught truth about their condition. Sometimes their deliverance will take a while because the person is unwilling to let go of the demonic personalities. If they are unwilling to let go of them, you are going to have to work with them over and over and over again. But if you persevere, you can get the job done. If they are desperate, it can happen quickly. By the time some people get to me, they have tried the worldly therapy, Christian therapy, secular psych hospitals, and even been into the Christian hospital programs. By this time their insurance and their money has run out, as well as their family's money. This reminds me of the woman in the Bible with the issue of blood.

> **Now a certain woman had a flow of blood for twelve years, [26] and <u>had suffered many things from many physicians. She had spent all that she had and was no better, but rather grew worse.</u> [27] When she heard about Jesus, she came behind *Him* in the crowd and touched His garment. [28] For she said, "If only I may touch His clothes, I shall be made well." [29] <u>Immediately the fountain of her blood was dried up, and she felt in *her* body that she was healed of the affliction.</u>**
>
> Mark 5:25-29

They might have even been to other deliverance ministries who were kind of "off-the-wall" and hurt them. And so, by the time they get to me, they are desperate. The more desperate they are, the quicker they will get their deliverance. If they are not real desperate, they may hang onto the lie, because they think it is safety.

If someone is suffering with MPD, they will be manifesting different personalities. You find out those names and break the soul-ties with them. Now when I say find out the names, you do not talk to the demons to find out names; you go by the names that are there. If the former names are a problem, break the soul-ties and cast out all illegal souls by those names. If your name is a shortened form of your name, and it is a problem, then do the same. After deliverance, you need to be called by your given name. This name thing is very important.

"We have a man in our church who has been delivered out of homosexuality. The name on his birth certificate is "Johnnie - the feminine form of the name; they evidently wanted a girl instead of a boy when he was born, so they feminized his name. As he was going through the process of deliverance, one of the things the Lord required him to do was to go back and officially have his name changed on his birth certificate to Johnny - the masculine form of the name." (7)

Nicknames - if you have a nickname that is a rebellious type name like "Tiger", "Rebel", etc, - and you have a terrible, mean attitude, then you need to break soul-ties with it and quit using it.

Then bind and cast out the spirit of "Tiger" or whatever. There is a problem if people keep speaking the name. It gives that spirit of "Tiger" legal rights, and the person takes on the attributes of a "Tiger" or whatever the name implies.

I saw an "Ernst" cartoon once where two huge guys were sitting on a bench reading the newspaper. Both of these guys were very obese; Ernst said to the other man, *"Hey, it says here that nicknames can have an effect on your life. What do you think about that, `Lardo'?"* Nicknames like that are spoken curses.

Question: *What about the name Junior?*

Answer: If someone is named Junior and you call them Junior that is fine. But if it's a nickname, you may have problems. It may cause that person to think of themselves as inferior and unable to measure up to others' standards. Therefore, they may have difficulty in growing up and taking responsibility.

Question: *What if your mother wanted to give you one name, but because of pressure, she named you something else; however, you hated that name all your life. Then when you were older, you started going by your middle name. Is that a problem?*

Answer: Your middle name is a given name. I have had some that it was a problem and some that weren't. The problem is not your middle name, but the rebellion. You have to go back to the reason the name was changed in the first place. There may be a problem with unforgiveness toward the person who talked your mother into changing the name. You will need to break all ungodly soul ties with them, forgive that person and your mom. By releasing them, you will be loosed from the problem. Then bind and cast out the spirits associated with that name.

"We had always known the lady that we received the schizophrenia revelation on, as Jean, which is her middle name. As she was getting her deliverance, she had to go back to her original name (Mary - Etta) which she had rebelled against." (8)

I have had people say, *"But all my stuff has this other name on it."* You need to break all soul-ties with that name and legally change all of that "stuff". They may be worried about the cost or the inconvenience. But God said we are not to covet the gold or anything, if it is something that is not of Him.

You shall burn the carved images of their gods with fire; <u>you shall not covet the silver or gold *that is* on them</u>, nor take *it* for yourselves, <u>lest you be snared by it</u>; for it *is* an abomination to the LORD** your God. 26Nor shall you bring an abomination into your house, lest you be doomed to destruction like it. <u>You shall utterly detest it and utterly abhor it</u>, for it *is* an accursed thing.   Deut. 7:25-26**

These different names will cause confusion and double-mindedness. You need to break the soul-ties and cast out the illegal souls, or you will have switching and checking out. If God can fearfully and wonderfully make you and call you from your mother's womb, He can surely figure out what to name you, can't He? What you, and other people, are speaking over you is very important.

NOTES: THE IMPORTANCE OF A NAME

6 James G. Friesen, Uncovering the Mystery of MPD ... (San Bernardino: Here's Life Publishers, 1991), 61

7 A verbal quote from Frank Hammond, author of "Pigs in the Parlor"

8 A verbal quote from Frank Hammond

MULTIPLE PERSONALITY DISORDER AND "ALTER PERSONALITIES"

With multiple personality disorder, there is a symptom therapists call *"alter personalities"*. Each personality will have a name and its own distinct set of mannerisms. Secular therapists will attempt to identify each one, acknowledge its strengths, and bring them all together to make one person. I do not believe that way nor attempt to communicate with these personalities.

Diagnostic criteria for 300.14 Multiple Personality Disorder

- A. The existence within the person of two or more distinct personalities or personality states (each with its own relatively enduring pattern of perceiving, relating to, and thinking about the environment and self).
- B. At least two of these personalities or personality states recurrently take full control of the person's behavior. (9)

Multiple Personality Disorder, Psychological or Demonic?

Secular psychiatry teaches that you need to know all the different names and that some of the personalities are good and some are bad. Several years ago, I went to a seminar on MPD and Satanic Ritual Abuse at a secular psychiatric hospital. The main speaker was a woman with a Ph.D. She was teaching about the traumatic events of Satanic Ritual Abuse that were causing dissociation. (I do agree with that.) At the beginning, she taught that all the alter personalities are liars. Later, she said there were good ones and bad ones, and you need to get the good ones on your side. The reason for doing that is so the good ones will tell you who the bad ones are, and what they are doing. At the end of her lecture, she opened the meeting for questions and answers. I said, *"Ma'am, I am just a little bit confused. A while ago you said that all the alters are liars. Now you say there are good ones and bad ones and you need to get the good ones on your side so they will expose the bad ones. Ma'am, if they are all liars, how can you tell when they are telling the truth or lying."* She looked a little flustered and said, *"Next question."* I let that one go by and sat there trying to behave. Finally, I raised my hand and asked her, *"If these are just alter personalities, where are the different voices coming from?"* She looked at me, looked at her watch, closed her notebook, said "I have to go", and walked out, it was over! That question ended the seminar, even though it was scheduled to last another half hour. In that seminar, the Ph.D said that as a therapist, you may work with a person for five or six years before you are able to diagnose them properly. Only then can you begin the process of therapy. I thought, *"Five or six years just to diagnose them?"* I couldn't believe what I was hearing.

Three or four months later, I went to a CAPS (Christian Association for Psychological Studies) meeting. It was a seminar with Jim Friesen, the author of **"Uncovering the Mystery of MPD"** and **"More than Survivors"**. I do not agree with all that he says in his book, but I had a little more hope with him. At least he acknowledges the demonic because he was coming from a Christian view. I do not agree with hypnotherapy, and I have a problem with his teaching that these are definitely alter personalities, that each alter personality may have demons, and that those demons may hide behind that personality. But I did like his acknowledgment that it would take about two and a half to three years to get these people straightened out. I said, "Well at least we have two and a half years knocked off." I came out of that with a little different understanding, but was still not satisfied in my own mind. Then the Lord started bringing people into my office and enrolled me in the "Holy Spirit School of MPD". We began to see people that psychiatrists would diagnose as multiple personalities. Within each of these people there were separate "personalities" with different names, voices, and attitudes. While working with these people under the leading of Holy Spirit, the Lord was bringing about amazing results.

God did not design man to be confused with 25 or 52 faces or personalities. Neither did He intend man to cope with distracting voices in our heads. He made us in His image and gave us a sound mind. Satan is the one who comes to "steal, kill, and destroy". We will look at God's design and plan in the next chapter.

NOTES: MULTIPLE PERSONALITY DISORDER AND "ALTER PERSONALITIES"

9 The American Psychiatric Association: Diagnostic and Statistical Manual of Mental Disorders, 3rd ed. (Washington, DC: American Psychiatric Association, 1987), 272.

THE THREE-FOLD BEING OF MAN

◖——◗

In Genesis God said, "*Let us make man in our image.*" Since God is a three-fold being - Father, Son, and Holy Spirit - then we need to understand that man also is a three-fold being. Man is <u>spirit</u>, possesses a <u>soul</u>, and lives in a <u>body</u>.

Paul referred to our three parts in scripture:

Now may the God of peace Himself sanctify you completely; and may your whole <u>spirit, soul, and body</u> be preserved blameless at the coming of our Lord Jesus Christ.   **1 Thessalonians 5:23**

In the New Testament, we are referred to as the temple of God:

Do you not know that you are the <u>temple of God</u> and *that* the Spirit of God dwells in you?
                                     1 Corinthians 3:16

Or do you not know that <u>your body is the temple of the Holy Spirit</u> *who is* in you, whom you have from God, and you are not your own?

1 Corinthians 6:19

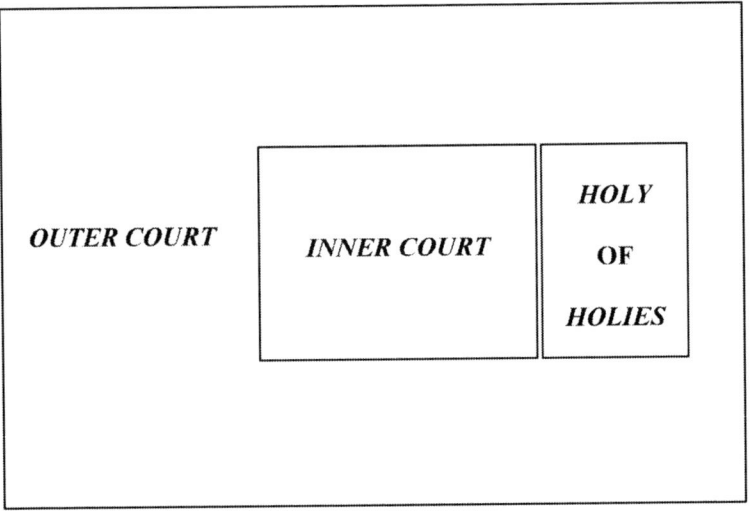

OLD TESTAMENT TEMPLE

Since we are the temple of God, we need to look at the temple in the Bible. The Old Testament temple had three parts: the outer court, the inner court, and the Holy of Holies. In the make-up of man, our flesh (body) is our "outer court", our soul (mind, will, and emotions) is our "inner court", and our spirit is our "Holy of Holies". God sat upon the Mercy Seat in the Holy of Holies in the Old Testament temple. At the foremost event of your salvation, when your spirit was born-again, the Spirit of God came to live in your Holy of Holies - your spirit. The born-again experience of salvation is an event.

> **Jesus answered and said to him, "Most assuredly, I say to you, unless one is <u>born again</u>, he cannot see the kingdom of God." John 3:3**

> *And it shall come to pass that whoever calls on the name of the LORD shall be <u>saved</u>.'* Acts 2:21

> **Nor is there <u>salvation</u> in any other, for there is no other name under heaven given among men by which we must be <u>saved</u>." Acts 4:12**

> <u>Saved</u>: sozo, Greek 4982, *sode'-zo*; from a primary sos (contracted for obsolete saos, "*safe*"); to *save*, i.e. *deliver* or *protect* (literal or figurative):- heal, preserve, save (self), do well, be (make) whole. Strong's (10)

The born-again experience is a spiritual reality, and it is our spirit that is born-again, not our soul. However, *Philippians 2:12* states, *"work out your own <u>salvation</u> with fear and trembling ..."*

> **Salvation: soteria, Greek 4991, *so-tay-ree'-ah*; feminine of a derivative of Greek 4990 (soter) as (properly**

abstract) noun; *rescue* **or** *safety* **(physical or morally): - deliver, health, salvation, save, saving. Strong's (11)**

But wait a minute, if salvation is being born-again and I am born-again, why do I have to work out my own salvation? Your spirit is born-again in the event, but there is a process of salvation also. The process is the renewing of your mind, will, and emotions - or the salvation of your soul - which involves discipline and deliverance. This is the process of sanctification.

I beseech you therefore, brethren, by the mercies of God, that you <u>present your bodies a living sacrifice</u>, holy, acceptable to God, *which is* **your reasonable service. ²And do not be conformed to this world, but <u>be transformed by the renewing of your mind</u>, that you may prove what** *is* **that good and acceptable and perfect will of God.**

Romans 12:1-2

Here, Paul is speaking of our body and our mind but does not mention our spirit. He is saying that as we work on these two parts to present them to God holy and acceptable, we will be in our right mind to discern the difference between the good and the perfect will of God for our lives. Paul does not mention our spirit because he was writing to born-again Christian saints in Rome.

... among whom <u>you also are the called of Jesus Christ</u>; ⁷To all who are in Rome, <u>beloved of God, called *to be* saints</u>: Grace to you and peace from God our Father and the Lord Jesus Christ.

Romans 1:6-7

When one is born-again, the Spirit of God is sitting on our mercy seat in our spirit-man - our "Holy of Holies". It doesn't get any better than that; there is no more work to be done on our spirit, only on our body and soul.

Now the just shall live by faith; but if anyone draws back, My soul has no pleasure in him." **³⁹But we are not of those who draw back to perdition, but of those <u>who believe to the saving of the soul</u>.**

Hebrews 10:38-39

<u>Soul</u>: psuche, Greek 5590, *psoo-khay'*; from Greek 5594 (psucho); *breath*, i.e. (by implication) *spirit*, abstract or concrete (the <u>*animal* sentient principle only</u>; thus <u>distinguished on the one hand from Greek 4151 (pneuma)</u>, which is the rational and immortal *soul*; and on the other from Greek 2222 (zoe), which is mere *vitality*, even of plants: these terms thus exactly correspond respectively to the Hebrew 5315 (nephesh), Hebrew 7307 (ruwach)

and Hebrew 2416 (chay)):- heart (+ -ily), life, mind, soul, + us, + you. Strong's (12)

Although this definition states that (**by implication**) a person's soul is spirit, it is not the person's spirit (pneuma). Let me explain: Man is a Spirit (pneuma) who possesses a Soul (psuche), and lives in a Body (soma). One's soul is their mind, will, and emotions. This definition calls soul as the "**animal sentient principle only**", and the American College Dictionary defines the sentient principle as "that part that feels; having the power of perception by the senses; the mind". These are not physical traits but abstract; therefore they are in the spiritual realm and not the physical, hence the implication of "spirit".

… so also in those passages where, in accordance with the trichotomy or threefold division of human nature by the Greeks, ηψυχη; is distinguished from το πνευμα - *pneuma* **(see πνευαμ, 2, p. 520a (and references under the word πνευμα 5)), <u>1 Thessalonians 5:23</u>; <u>Hebrews 4:12</u>.**

… "the seat of the feelings, desires, affections, aversions" (our "soul, heart," etc. (R.V. almost uniformly "soul"); … (13)

Now may the God of peace Himself sanctify you completely; and may your whole spirit, soul, and body be preserved blameless at the coming of our Lord Jesus Christ. 1 Thes. 5:23

For the word of God is living and powerful, and sharper than any two-edged sword, piercing even to the division of soul and spirit, and of joints and marrow, and is a discerner of the thoughts and intents of the heart.

Hebrews 4:12

This refers to a person's soul – the mind, will, and emotions. Demons enter in and build their strongholds in the soul and the flesh, but their main activity is in the soul. This corresponds with Dr. Friesen's components of dissociation that occur in the Mind, Emotions, Body, and Will in his Mesa Pattern of Clinical Expression of Dissociation chart on page 114 of "Uncovering the Mystery of MPD".

CLINICAL EXPRESSION OF DISSOCIATION
Mesa Pattern

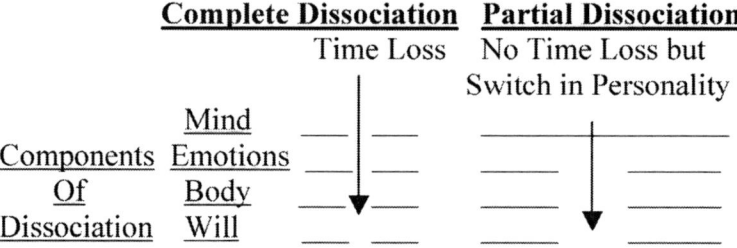

Let me remind you that even though a born-again Christian can have a demonic problem, they **cannot** be demon-possessed. **It is an impossibility for a born-again Christian to be demon-possessed!** Let me explain: The word for possessed in the King James Version of the Bible is a mistranslation. A better translation would be **"TO BE DEMONIZED"** or **"VEXED"** by a demon.

The translation of the Greek word is:

daimonizomai, Greek 1139, *dahee-mon-id'-zom-ahee*; **middle from Greek 1142 (daimon); to** *be exercised by a dæmon*:- **have a (be vexed with, be possessed with) devil (-s). Strong's (14)**

The definition of possession is: **to have and hold as property**. When a person is born-again, they have been **purchased with the blood of Jesus Christ and are now His possession**.

> **Therefore take heed to yourselves and to all the flock, among which the Holy Spirit has made you overseers, to shepherd the church of God which He purchased with His own blood.**
>
> **Acts 20:28**

> **Or do you not know that your body is the temple of the Holy Spirit** *who is* **in you, whom you have from God, and you are not your own? 20For you were bought at a price; therefore glorify God in your body and in your spirit, which are God's.**
>
> **1 Corinthians 6:19-20**

When one is possessed by Jesus Christ, it is an **impossibility to be possessed by a demon**. However, one can be **oppressed** by demons in our soul or body.

A person who has a problem with MPD will hear voices. The voices will tell them different things to keep them confused. Confusion is in the realm of the soul – mind, will, and emotions. Anyone who has worked in deliverance knows that demons will talk to you; but not all people who need deliverance hear voices, sometimes demons will only manifest through emotions and behaviors. Remember, we have been made in the **image of God** who is a **three-fold being**; thus **we are a three-fold being**. Since we are three-fold, then we do not have 16 or 25 or 52 faces. We have a spirit, a soul, and a body. God did not make us with multiple personalities. According to Psalms 139, God has fearfully and wonderfully made us.

> For **You formed my inward parts**; You covered me in my mother's womb. ^{14}I will praise You, for **I am fearfully *and* wonderfully made**; marvelous are Your works, and *that* my soul knows very well. ^{15}**My frame was not hidden from You**, when I was made in secret, a*nd* **skillfully wrought in the lowest parts of the earth**. ^{16}Your eyes saw my substance, being yet unformed. And in Your book they all were written, the days fashioned for me, when *as yet there were* none of them.
>
> **Psalm 139:13-16**

While working with people, we need to keep in mind that **God created them good** and there is **nothing impossible with God**. Our residential treatment center is a part of **Restore To More Ministries**; and God's desire for people is to "**restore them to more**" than they were.

NOTES: THE THREE-FOLD BEING OF MAN

10 James Strong, Strong's Exhaustive Concordance: Compact Edition, (Grand Rapids: Baker Book House, 1982), 880

11 Ibid, 874

12 Ibid, 961

13 Joseph H. Thayer, Thayer's Greek-English Lexicon of the New Testament: 4th Edition, (Grand Rapids: Baker Book House, 1977), 677

14 (James Strong), 800

A BIBLICAL CASE OF MULTIPLE PERSONALITY

DEMONIAC – MULTIPLE

I want us to take a look at an example from the Bible that I believe exhibits multiple personality traits. The demoniac in the Gadarenes, in Mark 5:1-19, presented characteristic patterns and social illnesses that often accompany a person with this malady. His personality was being eclipsed by something else.

> **"In demonization the personality of the demon eclipses the personality of the person afflicted. The demon displays his personality through the human's body to a greater or lesser degree. The control may be overt or covert." (15)**

I believe in this case it was a "nest of demons" that presented itself as a personality who spoke with one voice as "Legion", representing them all.

Multiple Personality Disorder, Psychological or Demonic?

Then they came to the other side of the sea, to the country of the Gadarenes. ²And when He had come out of the boat, immediately there met Him out of the tombs a man with an unclean spirit, ³who had *his* dwelling among the tombs; and no one could bind him, not even with chains, ⁴because he had often been bound with shackles and chains. And the chains had been pulled apart by him, and the shackles broken in pieces; neither could anyone tame him. ⁵And always, night and day, <u>he was in the mountains and in the tombs, crying out and cutting himself with stones</u>.

Mark 5:1-5

This shows the social pathological behaviors of avoidance, isolation, and self-mutilation. I have witnessed these symptoms in multiple personality patients.

⁶<u>When he saw Jesus from afar, he ran and worshiped Him.</u>

This was the real man who recognized Jesus as one who could help him. He made a conscious decision to run toward Jesus and worship Him. He was presenting himself to Jesus for ministry, to be set free from the torment of another personality doing what he did not want to do. But he was overshadowed by another one.

7And he cried out with a loud voice and said, "What have I to do with You, Jesus, Son of the Most High God? I implore You by God that You <u>do not torment me</u>." 8For He said to him, "Come out of the man, unclean spirit!"

The real man worshiped Jesus and presented himself for ministry. Therefore, it was not him who was speaking at this time; he was not fearful that Jesus was going to torment him. It was the demonic personality that overshadowed him speaking.

9Then He asked him, "What *is* your name?"

At this time, Jesus was speaking to the man. There are times during ministry when the person I am ministering to will lose contact with the present. They will take on a blank look or change to a different voice and not understand what we are doing. At that time, I will speak to the person and say, "In the name of Jesus, I speak to the spirit of (their real name) to rise up and come into agreement with me." What I am doing is getting them to use all their faculties to come into agreement with me; and not let the demonic ruin the ministry session. I need their agreement, and God's help, to have a successful ministry session. The Bible says:

> **Again I say to you that if <u>two of you agree on earth concerning anything</u> that they ask, <u>it will be done for them by My Father in heaven</u>.**
>
> Matthew 18:19

The demonic personality spoke with one voice representing many demons that were controlling the man. This was not the real person speaking at this time.

> **And he answered, saying, "<u>My</u> name *is* Legion; for <u>we are many</u>." ¹⁰Also he begged Him earnestly that He would not send them out of the country. ¹¹Now a large herd of swine was feeding there near the mountains. ¹²So all the demons begged Him, saying, "Send us to the swine, that we may enter them." ¹³And at once Jesus gave them permission. Then the unclean spirits went out and entered the swine (there were about two thousand); and the herd ran violently down the steep place into the sea, and drowned in the sea. ¹⁴So those who fed the swine fled, and they told *it* in the city and in the country. And they went out to see what it was that had happened. ¹⁵Then they came to Jesus, and saw the one *who had been* demon-possessed and had the legion, sitting and clothed and <u>in his right mind.</u>**

When the demonic personality, or nest of demons, identified as "Legion" was expelled, the man was able to sit peacefully and carry on a conversation in his right mind.

And they were afraid. 16And those who saw it told them how it happened to him *who had been* demon-possessed, and about the swine. 17Then they began to plead with Him to depart from their region. 18And when He got into the boat, he who had been demon-possessed begged Him that he might be with Him. 19However, Jesus did not permit him, but said to him, "Go home to your friends, and tell them what great things the Lord has done for you, and how He has had compassion on you."

Mark 5:1-19

I believe this is in the Bible to allow us to understand the power we have been given in the use of the Name of Jesus.

For where two or three are gathered together <u>in My name</u>, I am there in the midst of them."

Matthew 18:20

And these signs will follow those who believe: <u>In My name they will cast out demons</u>; they will speak with new tongues;

Mark 16:17

"Most assuredly, I say to you, he who believes in Me, the works that I do he will do also; and greater *works* than these he will do, because I go to My Father. ¹³And <u>whatever you ask in My name</u>, that <u>I will do</u>, that the Father may be glorified in the Son. ¹⁴<u>If you ask anything in My name, I will do</u> *it*. John 14:12-14

"Legion" is a Roman military term designating a regiment that consisted of 3,000 to 6,000 infantrymen, plus the Calvary and Artillery!

legeon, Greek 3003; *leg-eh-ohn'***; of Latin origin; a "***legion***", i.e. Roman** *regiment* **(figurative):- legion. Strong's (16)**

This man had upwards of 6,000 demons that Jesus dealt with using only spiritual authority, words, and Holy Ghost power. In today's social climate, this man in the Gaderenes would definitely be diagnosed with a psychotic mental disorder and admitted to a hospital equipped to deal with one so severely handicapped. Throughout the history of psychology, he may have been restrained mechanically, treated with malaria (Jauregg), given electroshock therapy (Cerletti & Bini), given lithium (Cade), chloropromazine (Delay & Deneker), or a host of other drugs, or even a lobotomy; but

Jesus dealt with this man on the spiritual level, and within minutes he was dressed and in his right mind.

NOTES: A BIBLICAL CASE OF MULTIPLE PERSONALITY

DEMONIAC – MULTIPLE

15 Fred Dickason, Demon Possession and the Christian: A New Perspective (Chicago: Moody Press, 1987), 41.

16 James Strong, Strong's Exhaustive Concordance: Compact Edition, (Grand Rapids: Baker Book House, 1982), 592.

DISSOCIATION

"The noun, dissociation, is the act of defending against pain. It may be the most effective defense people can use, since it is 100 percent successful. When a person dissociates, he or she separates from the memory of a painful event." (17)

Psychiatry teaches that "multiples" are formed whenever a person dissociates. What causes dissociation? Dissociation can happen when there is a traumatic event in a person's life. It may be from satanic ritual abuse or even repetitious abuse. It can be any abuse - physical, sexual or even mental. This could even happen from a one-time event, if it is traumatic enough. It does not have to be repetitious. Dissociation happens whenever the person's emotions cannot handle the situation. When someone goes through trauma, especially repetitious, eventually the mind snaps. When that happens, the mind escapes to another place that seems to be safer.

Dissociation is a basic defense mechanism that is employed to protect a person's sanity.

> **"It is as simple as this: A child goes through a trauma, and then pretends to be a new person, or alternate personality (alter), to whom those bad things did not happen. There is a separation from the memory. It is immediately and completely forgotten. The newly created alter "remembers" only a blank spot where the trauma happened, and there is no hint that the traumatic event could have happened. If the dissociation is complete, the amnesia is 100 percent. If you mention anything about what happened during the blank spot, there is a puzzled look on the new alter's face: "I have no idea what you are talking about." (18)**

This seems to be a good mechanism at the time to prevent a more serious problem; and it appears to be "safe". The problems arise later in life when the memories begin to surface and it "feels like I am losing my mind".

FIGURE 3

EMOTIONS GRADUATION SCALE

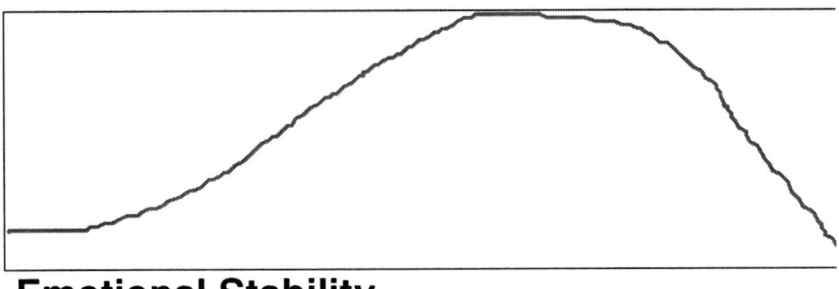

Emotional Stability

The curved line in **Figure 3** illustrates our normal emotional reaction to an event: our emotions usually will build up gradually and then recede to a normal emotional level. But during a traumatic event, repetitious or not, when the fear and hopelessness becomes too much, dissociation happens. Because they are holding in their emotions, the person may be like an emotional flat liner, but when they snap, their emotions will abruptly shoot up like **Figure 4**. This is the point of dissociation, and a new personality or multiple personalities will begin to form.

FIGURE 4

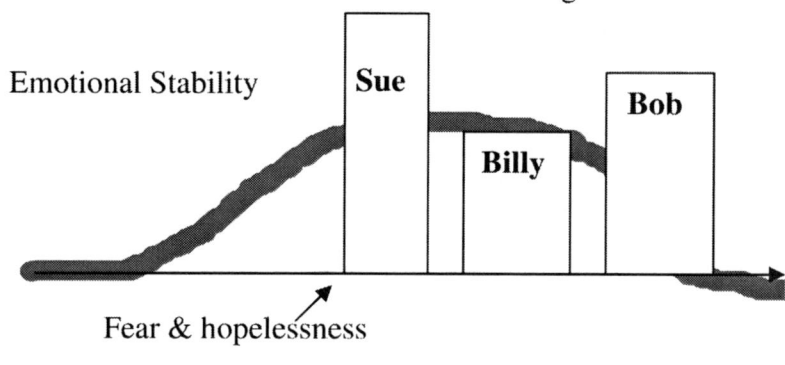

When someone dissociates during abuse or a traumatic event or events, they are utilizing a survival technique. When a person is suffering through satanic ritual abuse or repetitious abuse, there are usually threats to keep them quiet. Some have been forced to take a vow of silence, with threats that they, or someone they love, will be hurt or even killed. They can't say or do anything, so they bottle it all up and hold it inside. When someone experiences traumatic events and holds in his emotions, instead of having the normal ebb and flow of emotions (**Figure 3**) suddenly he will snap and dissociate. He will think, usually a sub-conscious thought, "It's not getting any better, and it doesn't look like it will ever get any better; I can't handle this." There is tremendous fear and hopelessness, and he will "check out" or dissociate (**Figure 4**). This is when psychiatry says an alter personality is formed. I believe this is when a spirit comes to deceive the person and promises to take away the pain and help them if the person will give it authority in their life, (**see Figure 5**). This is similar to what Satan did with Adam and Eve in the Garden of Eden. Eve was deceived; Satan promised rewards if they did what he said. Eve responded; and Adam gave up his authority, so he would not suffer (separation from his woman). Demonic spirits promise to do something that sounds good for us, but it is really done for Satan's advantage.

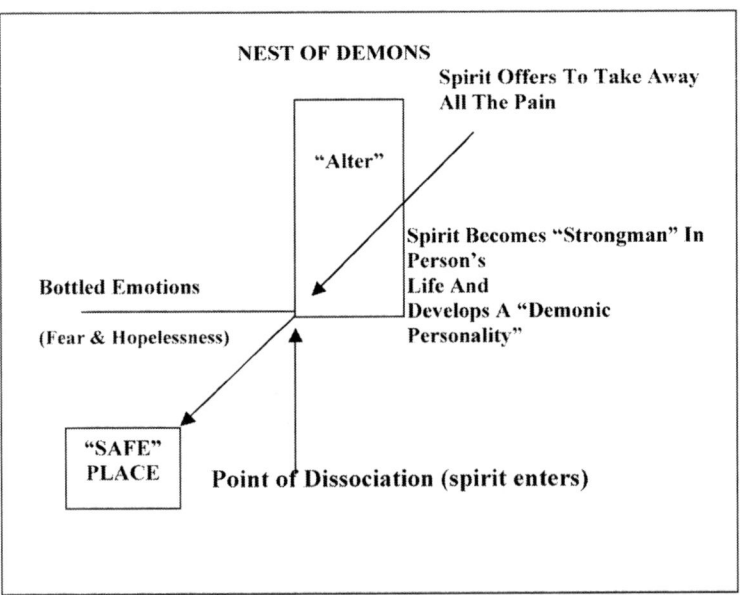

FIGURE 5

I have learned through experience that at the point of tremendous fear and hopelessness the person escapes in their mind to what they think is a "safe place". A voice will promise them that it will not hurt any more (escape from the pain), and they dissociate. They avoid the pain, but instead of it turning into a good thing, a demon comes in to build a stronghold or demonic personality. At this time, this demon becomes the "strong man" in the person.

No one can enter a strong man's house and plunder his goods, unless he first binds the <u>strong man</u>. And then he will plunder his house.   **Mark 3:27**

This is not a part of the person, but a demon that has entered deceitfully and set up a stronghold from which to rule in this person's life. He then begins to develop a team or "nest" of demons to sabotage and destroy this person's peace of mind. I want to remind everyone that fear and hopelessness is demonic and God did not give us a spirit of fear.

For God has not given us a spirit of fear, but of power and of love and of a sound mind.   **2 Timothy 1:7**

So we see that this dissociation was started demonically. Therefore, everything that is produced from this point on is demonic. When dealing with someone like this, if you will lead them in a prayer to break every vow of silence, and then let them know that it is all right to tell what happened to them, sometimes it will release their memories right then. Then, you can begin to work towards their deliverance. I am not saying they will be delivered this quickly; unless Holy Spirit does a miraculous deliverance, it will take longer. It depends a lot on the trust level between the person and the minister and the support system that is in place. Do not allow any condemnation towards anyone who is suffering through this type of situation.

<u>Little by little I will drive them out</u> from before you, <u>until you have increased</u>, and you inherit (possess) the land.
                                                                                      Exodus 23:30

"When an unclean spirit goes out of a man, he goes through dry places, seeking rest, and finds none. ⁴⁴ Then he says, 'I will return to my house from which I came.' And when he comes, <u>he finds *it* empty</u>, swept, and put in order. ⁴⁵ Then he goes and takes with him seven other spirits more wicked than himself, and they enter and dwell there; and <u>the last *state* of that man is worse than the first</u>. ..."   Matthew 12:43-45

These Old and New Testament scriptures each tell of how God is concerned about our growth and our ability to maintain the deliverance He brings. In Exodus He is talking about physical enemies of the Israelites; but in Matthew He is talking of spiritual enemies we face today. The importance stressed in both scriptures is how we must have the Spirit of the Lord within us (so as not to be empty), and increase in spiritual wisdom so that we can possess the land (our spirit, soul, and body). Freedom from oppression takes time – the more one digs into the Word of God and matures and trusts God and the minister – the quicker the freedom.

When working with someone, I will explain about trauma and dissociation. Then I explain how I will ask Holy Spirit to take them back in their memories to the point of origin of the lie they believed. Holy Spirit knows everything and can reveal truth in a non-threatening way. I tell them not to be afraid of the past, but to allow Holy Spirit to comfort them in the pain. He knows everything about their life, and He is the true comforter who wants to heal their hurt. Then I ask them to relax while I pray and ask Holy Spirit to take them back and speak truth into the situation.

> **But the <u>Comforter</u>, which is <u>the Holy Ghost</u>, whom the Father will send in my name, he shall teach you all things, and <u>bring all things to your remembrance</u>, whatsoever I have said unto you. [27] Peace I leave with you, <u>my peace I give unto you:</u> not as the world giveth, give I unto you. <u>Let not your heart be troubled, neither let it be afraid.</u>**
>
> **John 14:26-27 (KJV)**

It is amazing when Holy Spirit works and they have a release of their emotions. I have seen tremendous freedom in a short time with this. They will still have the memory, but the pain and fear are gone.

Because of the things I have experienced, I believe that what psychiatry calls an "alter personality" is really a nest of demons. Each nest of demons may go by either a masculine or a feminine name and display all the corresponding character traits. Psychiatry would have this person map out the dates and times that each "personality" entered their life and what caused them to come in. You get one here, one over here, and one over there, and then you connect them all. **(See Figure 6)**

PERSONALITY MAP

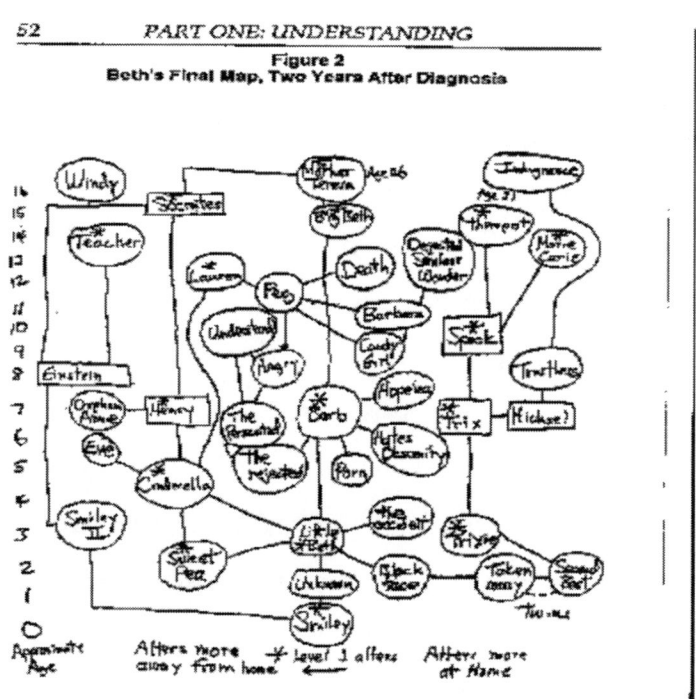

FIGURE 6

Figure 6 is from "Uncovering the Mystery of MPD" by Dr. James Friesen. I used his illustration because I do not have clients "map" out personalities. I believe they are demonic, and I do not speak to or interrogate demons. Jesus is our example and He never questioned them or allowed them to speak; but told them to be quiet.

But Jesus rebuked him, saying, "Be quiet, and come out of him!" **Mark 1:25**

Then He healed many who were sick with various diseases, and cast out many demons; and He did not allow the demons to speak, because they knew Him.
Mark 1:34

When we question demons and allow them to speak, we are letting a demon direct the ministry. This is not biblical, nor wise. Demons are liars and deceivers and cannot be trusted.

You are of your father the devil, and the desires of your father you want to do. He was a murderer from the beginning, and does not stand in the truth, because there is no truth in him. When he speaks a lie, he speaks from his own resources, for he is a liar and the father of it.
John 8:44

We have access to all truth and power through the manifestations of the Holy Spirit.

And I will pray the Father, and He will give you another Helper, that He may abide with you forever— [17] the Spirit of truth, whom the world cannot receive, because

it neither sees Him nor knows Him; but you know Him, for **He dwells with you and will be in you.** John 14:16-17

But **the Helper, the Holy Spirit**, whom the Father will send in My name, **He will teach you all things**, and bring to your remembrance all things that I said to you.
John 14:26

However, when **He, the Spirit of truth**, has come, **He will guide you into all truth**; for He will not speak on His own authority, but whatever He hears He will speak; and He will tell you things to come. John 16:13

But **you shall receive power when the Holy Spirit has come upon you**; and you shall be witnesses to Me in Jerusalem, and in all Judea and Samaria, and to the end of the earth." Acts 1:8

But **the manifestation of the Spirit is given to each one for the profit of all**: [8] for to one is given the **word of wisdom** through the Spirit, to another the **word of knowledge** through the same Spirit, [9] to another faith by the same Spirit, to another **gifts of healings** by the same Spirit, [10] to another the working of miracles, to another **prophecy**, to another **discerning of spirits**, to another different kinds

of tongues, to another the interpretation of tongues. [11] But one and the same Spirit works all these things, distributing to each one individually as He wills.

1 Corinthians 12:7-11

Interrogating demons can lead one to becoming a consulter with familiar spirits, which is strictly forbidden in the scriptures.

'A <u>man or a woman</u> who is a medium, or <u>who has familiar spirits</u>, shall <u>surely be put to death; they shall stone them with stones</u>. Their blood shall be upon them.'

Leviticus 20:27

So <u>Saul died for his transgression</u> which he committed against the LORD, *even* **against the word of the LORD, which he kept not, and also <u>for asking</u>** *<u>counsel</u>* **<u>of</u>** *<u>one that had</u>* **<u>a familiar spirit, to enquire</u>** *<u>of it</u>***;**

1 Chronicles 10:13 (KJV)

Relying on demons for insight about a person's life is turning away from God, departing from the faith, and giving heed to deceiving spirits. I will rely upon Holy Spirit to direct the ministry, not listen to doctrines of demons.

Now the Spirit expressly says that in latter times some will depart from the faith, <u>giving heed to deceiving spirits and doctrines of demons</u>, 1 Tim. 4:1

An "alter personality" is really a nest of demons that will go by a different name. Each one will speak with a different voice. If, according to psychiatry, this is a personality, then let's look again at what psychiatry considers a personality.

"Personality traits are enduring patterns of perceiving, relating to, and thinking about the environment and one self (*sic*), and are exhibited in a wide range of important social and personal contexts." (19)

Personality: Psycholog. "All the constitutional, mental, emotional, social, etc. characteristics of an individual. An organized pattern of all the characteristics of an individual." (20)

Dickason has stated his beliefs of how demons will eclipse a person's true personality.

Demonization is always presented as a spirit's inhabiting a human. This is evidenced by the expression such as "for many demons had entered him". Here the spirit

who is external to the man is seen as invading his body, most likely the control centers of the brain that affect his mind, behavior, and physical strength. (21)

Jesus asked him, saying, "What is your name?" And he said, "Legion," <u>because many demons had entered him</u>.

Luke 8:30

"In demonization the personality of the demon eclipses the personality of the person afflicted. The demon displays his personality through the human's body to a greater or lesser degree. The control may be overt or covert." (22)

The phenomenon of demonization surpasses scientific and psychological explanation. It is marked *<u>by the influence of a demon personality</u>* within a human with certain rather well-defined characteristics – a demonic syndrome obvious in Scripture and in case studies today. (23)

<u>Italics and underline added by this author</u>

Let us take a look at scriptural demonstrations of how demonic influence causes a person to manifest different personalities.

"Lord, have mercy on my son," he said. "<u>He has seizures and is suffering greatly</u>. He often <u>falls into the fire or into the water</u>.   Matthew 17:15 (NIV)

A <u>spirit seizes him</u> and <u>he suddenly screams</u>; it throws him into <u>convulsions so that he foams at the mouth</u>. It scarcely ever leaves him and is destroying him.
                              Luke 9:39 (NIV)

Then they brought to Him one <u>who was deaf and had an impediment in his speech</u>, and they begged Him to put His hand on him.   Mark 7:32

And when He had come out of the boat, immediately there met Him out of the tombs <u>a man with an unclean spirit</u>, [3] who had his <u>dwelling among the tombs</u>; and no one could bind him, not even with chains, [4] because he had often been bound with shackles and chains. And the <u>chains had been pulled apart</u> by him, and the <u>shackles broken in pieces</u>; <u>neither could anyone tame him</u>. [5] And always, night and day, he was <u>in the mountains and in the tombs, crying out and cutting himself with stones</u>.
                              Mark 5:2-5

Does that sound like ways of presenting oneself and making an impression on others? These quotes from the Bible illustrate how demons invade and develop strongholds in people's lives.

In the fifth chapter of the Gospel of Mark, the person was displaying characteristics that were not his own, but the demons'. Jesus cast the legion of demons out of the man in the Gadarenes, and then he was dressed and in his right mind. In the case of the boy who couldn't speak or hear, Jesus cast the demon out, and then the boy could both talk and hear. In the case of the boy who was thrown on the ground and foaming at the mouth, Jesus rebuked the demon and the boy was immediately healed. Jesus laid His hands on the woman who was bent low for eighteen years by a spirit of infirmity, and immediately, she straightened up and praised the Lord.

> **"And when he stepped out on the land, there met Him a certain man from the city who had demons for a long time. And he wore no clothes, nor did he live in a house but in the tombs. When he saw Jesus, he cried out, fell down before Him, and with a loud voice, said, "What do I have to do with you, Jesus, Son of the Most High God? I beg you, do not torture me!" <u>For He had commanded the unclean spirit to come out of the man</u>. For it often seized him, and he broke the bonds and was driven by the demon into the wilderness."**
>
> **Luke 8:27-29**

Multiple Personality Disorder, Psychological or Demonic?

When Jesus spoke to these demons, they were speaking, shouting, and begging, and they were afraid of being tortured; but also they were obedient to Jesus' authority. Shouting, screaming, begging, pleading, and showing fear are characteristics of a personality. These were personality characteristics being displayed by demons, not the man. When Jesus rebuked and cast out the nest of demons called Legion, the man was in his right mind and dressed properly. The demons were exercising their characteristics over the person's own personality characteristics.

> "In the case of the Gadarene, on the one hand, he runs to Jesus, apparently for help. On the other hand, he reacts in fear and begs Him not to torment him. <u>There is an obvious visible and terrible conflict within the demonized person. He never knows from one moment to the next when the powers of darkness will choose to take over and black out his personality</u>." (24)

"The new interjected personality enables the severely demonized person to speak with other voices that are not his own and in languages he has never studied. It is a common occurrence for a woman in the demonized state to speak with the deep bass of a man's voice or a man to speak with a woman's voice. It is not unusual for a severely demonized person to speak with many voices, for each demon may speak out by using the victim's tongue and vocal cords. **<u>But the amazing thing is that the new personality (or personalities, as the case may be)</u>** often speaks languages completely unknown to the victim." (25)

<u>Italics and underline added by this author</u>

We did not fully see the real man in the issue of the Gadarene demoniac until the demons were cast out. Then the real man wanted to serve God; because he begged to go with Jesus.

And when He got into the boat, he who had been demon-possessed <u>begged Him that he might be with Him</u>. 19However, Jesus did not permit him, but said to him, "Go home to your friends, and tell them what great things the Lord has done for you, and how He has had compassion on you." 20And he departed and began to proclaim in Decapolis all that Jesus had done for him; and all marveled.   **Mark 5:18-20**

There are a lot of people in this world that secular, even some Christian, therapists are hurting. These people are hurting and suffering while the so-called "helpers" are trying to get things straightened out by talking to demons. Talking to the demons within them will never help people. I have worked with people who have been in psychiatric hospital after hospital and through all types of therapy. But when they go through deliverance, the captives are set free. I am not saying that you do not have to talk to people to find out the traumas they have encountered in life. When working with someone, one must be aware of these situations and the person's life and traumas cannot be trivialized. I will ask the Lord to take them back to the memories and deal with them at that time in their life. When God heals and delivers them, I do not need to know all the gory details.

I believe memories are containers of information, some are open and good, but some contain lies that the person believed at that time. The lies were inspired by demonic events, then perpetuated and guarded by demons. The demons will erect walls around these memories, then they become strongholds in the person's life. One must use divinely empowered spiritual weapons when dealing with these strongholds.

> **For though we walk in the flesh, <u>we do not war according to the flesh</u>. 4For <u>the weapons of our warfare *are* not carnal but mighty in God for pulling down strongholds</u>, 5casting down arguments and every high thing that exalts itself against the knowledge of God, bringing every thought into captivity to the obedience of Christ,**
>
> **2 Corinthians 10:3-5**

Multiple Personality Disorder, Psychological or Demonic?

I think demons tolerate (maybe they are even amused by) therapists who only ask questions using psychiatry and psychology methods. I believe God led me to get the Master's Degree and all the academic courses to be a Licensed Professional Counselor, so I would have the background. But, I believe He told me not to get the State of Texas and humanistic techniques involved in the ministry.

Vines Dictionary states the definition of "daimonizomai", the Greek word used for the translation of "demon-possessed" in the King James Version of the Bible, as:

"daimonizomai" **signifies to be possessed of a demon, to act under the control of a demon. *Those who were thus afflicted expressed the mind and consciousness of the demon or demons indwelling them."* (26)

Italics and underline added by this author

That means that whenever a demon comes into someone, the demon begins to display his own characteristics. Then the person cannot express his true personality traits because the demon(s) is eclipsing the personality of the person. What people are seeing and hearing is the **demonic personality**, not alter personalities! Instead of calling these things alter personalities, let's call them by what they really are - a nest of manifesting demons. The objective is not just to cast out a demon, but to get rid of the whole nest of demons who are displaying personality traits.

Multiple Personality Disorder, Psychological or Demonic?

These nests of demons will interact with each other to form a system. You may have a nest of them over here that are calling themselves Joe and another nest over here that goes by the name of Phyllis, or whatever. You may have several other nests, but be assured of this; **no demonic personality has more power or authority than someone who operates in the authority of the name of Jesus!!** I have had some manifest in my office, and they sure can say some rude things. Then, I have had some people come in and not even be able to talk.

One lady came to the church while I was in a session with someone else. My wife, Geneva, greeted her in the sanctuary of the church. The woman told us later that those demons told her, *"That little gal can't help you. You might as well leave."* But my wife (5'2") sat her down and bound the demons. It was as if my wife had handcuffed her in the chair. The lady sat there, and my wife continued working and praying under her breath, while waiting for me to finish my other appointment.

When I was done, Geneva came over and said, *"Phillip, I think we need you in here."* When I walked into Geneva's office, the demons were bound; the lady could not talk, and was looking down at the floor. When I made her look at me, she tried to bolt out of that chair and hide underneath another chair. I just bound the demons and said, *"No! Sit down."* After some deliverance, the lady was able to talk. This lady told us that whenever the demons saw me, they screamed in her mind. They hated me walking into the room. Was that an alter personality or does that sound like something out of the Bible?

> **And he cried out with a loud voice and said, "What have I to do with You, Jesus, Son of the Most High God? <u>I implore You by God that You do not torment me</u>."**
>
> **Mark 5:7**

The demons were not afraid of me personally, but demons recognize one who is walking in the authority of the Name of Jesus, and they do not like it.

> **Then some of the itinerant Jewish exorcists took it upon themselves to call the name of the Lord Jesus over those who had evil spirits, saying, "We exorcise you <u>by the Jesus whom Paul preaches</u>." 14Also there were seven sons of Sceva, a Jewish chief priest, who did so. 15And the evil spirit answered and said, "<u>Jesus I know, and Paul I know; but who are you?</u>" 16Then the man in whom the evil spirit was leaped on them, overpowered them, and prevailed against them, so that they fled out of that house naked and wounded.**
>
> **Acts 19:13-16**

Demons know who is operating in the authority of the Name of Jesus, and they know **if you know** you have that authority. We have those types of situations often in our ministry.

NOTES: DISSOCIATION

17 James G. Friesen, Uncovering the Mystery of MPD: Its Shocking Origins ... Its Surprising Cure (San Bernardino: Here's Life Publishers, 1991), 62.

18 Ibid, 63.

19 The American Psychiatric Association: Diagnostic and Statistical Manual of Mental Disorders, 3rd ed. (Washington, DC: American Psychiatric Association, 1987), 335.

20 Barnhart, C. L. & Jess Stein, eds, American College Dictionary, (New York: Random House, 1967), 904.

21 Fred C. Dickason, Demon Possession and the Christian: A New Perspective (Chicago: Moody Press, 1987), 40.

22 Ibid, 41.

23 Ibid, 47.

24 Merrill F. Unger, What Demons Can Do To Saints (Chicago: Moody Press, 1991), 144.

25 Ibid, 144.

26 W. E. Vine, Vine's Expository Dictionary of Old and New Testament Words (New Jersey: Fleming H. Revell Company, 1981), 291.

DISSOCIATION AND AMNESIA

◧ — ◨

A lot of people who dissociate suffer from amnesia.

> **"Dissociation is the most wonderful protection against pain that any child could ever develop. There could be no more effective defense – the child pretends the traumatic event happened to somebody else, and then ... Poof! ... COMPLETELY forgets about it. It is gone." (27)**

To the degree of how much and how often they "checked out", will be the degree of amnesia. They will have amnesia because a demon came along and promised to help them by taking away the pain. They gave it authority in their life and then "escaped" to a so-called "safe place" in their mind. The demon then took over and started developing a demonic personality; the real person does not remember what happened after that. In total amnesia there is a time loss. There will be segments of time that people just can't remember. Other people won't have a total time loss, but will suffer partial amnesia. They can remember major parts, but not too many details.

Below is Dr. Friesen's chart showing the difference between complete and partial dissociation. Essentially, the only difference is with partial dissociation there is no time loss. In other words, the person will switch in personality, but with no amnesia.

CLINICAL EXPRESSION OF DISSOCIATION
Mesa Pattern

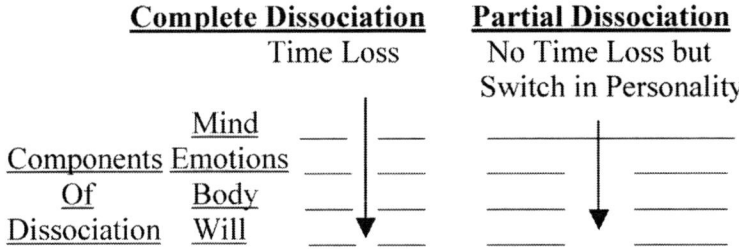

Some people go through life seemingly without difficulty, and then something will happen that will trigger a memory of something and they will flip out. It is a memory of the trauma and/or abuse and it shocks them. Then they begin to have flashbacks, dreams, or visions of things that happened to them as a child, but because they had checked out, they never had the memories before. Now that they are starting to remember, it scares them and may even cause them to think they are going crazy. Sometimes the memories will come as pain in different parts of the body; this is known as a "**body**

memory." A lot of times the person will have tremendous pain in their sexual organs. Then with that pain, they will have a flash back. It is not a "body-memory"; it is a demon manifesting. That one lady I told you about with all the names from previous marriages, she was also having painful manifestations. The demon that entered in during the childhood abuse was beginning to manifest in the same point of entry of the abuse as a child.

> **One particular partial dissociation was described in chapter 2, where the client told me her body remembered what it was like to have sex, but her mind did not. In that case, only the bodily memory had been accessed during therapy, while the other components remained dissociated. Many times during a therapy session, a partial dissociation is recovered, and usually it is the bodily memory. Too often it is quite disconcerting, and even embarrassing for the client, because his or her body starts reacting without the mind knowing what the body's reaction means. (28)**

The demons will lie dormant and then manifest where the abuse happened. If it was sexual abuse and there was a lot of pain to that child, the demon that came in to the sexual organs will begin to manifest again after many years. If there was physical abuse with beatings, it may manifest in the back where they were beaten. This **"body-memory"** is, in reality, a demon manifesting.

One girl in Illinois who I worked with suffered with total amnesia. The following is an account of her deliverance and parts of her life that she related to me.

L_____'s Testimony: Her mom and dad are in a witch's coven in Chicago. He is a high priest of Satan, her mom is a priestess of Satan, and this girl had been a priestess at one time. While growing up, she went through extreme mental, physical, and sexual abuse from her parents and the coven. One punishment that was inflicted, if she didn't do what her parents told her to do, was to put her in a hole in the back yard, close the lid over her, and leave her there for three days. She was frequently drugged and made to perform in pornographic movies. They wanted her to have sex with her puppy in one of the pornographic movies, but she refused. They chopped the dog into pieces and then put it on top of her inside a closed casket for three days. They drugged her frequently and made her perform Satanic rituals during her childhood. She went to a Catholic school, and the monsignor of the Catholic school was a part of the witch's coven. They would take her out of school to go do these things, but on her records she had perfect grades and perfect attendance. However, she had to teach herself how to read by using a flashlight under the covers of her bed. At 12 years old, she was impregnated by her dad and made to sacrifice the baby by skinning it alive. This is when he received his rank of high priest and she became a priestess. She was a programmed "destroyer". Satanists will send a "destroyer" into a church to sow discord, distrust, and strife among the members. If the members do not spiritually discern what is happening and deal with it in the spirit-realm, the church will be destroyed from within. Then the "destroyer" will have accomplished his/her task and will leave quietly.

The church she attended flew me to Illinois to work with her. What I found when I arrived was a nine-year old child in a 24-year-old woman's body. She had dissociated, and in her mind she was nine years old. Some of the "demonic personalities" that were in her were: Valerie, Michelle, Diamond, Vicki, Amy, Susie, Rebecca, Slut, Bitch, Little Demon, Mary, Crazy, Stupid, and Trouble.

We worked with her for fourteen hours. About two o'clock in the afternoon, we had a breakthrough and she returned to fourteen years of age. At about ten that night, she came back to 24 years old, but we still had problems.

There were trigger words that had been planted in her. Every time she heard those words, she would dissociate. The fact that she had accepted Jesus Christ and was born-again is a miracle because **CHRIST** and **SAVED** were two of those trigger words. The leader of the coven had programmed her to check out if someone tried to lead her in a sinner's prayer. It was a miracle of God that she was born again; but then it was a miracle of grace for any of us to be saved, wasn't it? I knew those trigger words because she had been living with a family from that church for five months. When they started realizing what she was doing, they began writing down the words that had been said when she dissociated. They had compiled a list of 20+ words. Around midnight, I gave her the list of words and she read the whole list without any problems. Plus there were certain objects, one being a balloon, which would cause her to dissociate. The bed in one of the porno movies was lined with balloons. This particular movie was a snuff film in which a man had been shot and killed. So every time she saw a balloon, she would check out and dissociate. After she read the list of words, the family with whom she lived mentioned the balloon and wondered if this would still cause her trouble. So we brought a balloon into the room; and as soon as she saw the balloon we lost her, she checked out. By the time we left that night, around 2:00 AM, she was playing with that balloon, Praise God!!

When she would "check out", I would tell the spirit of L____ (her real name) to rise up strong in the name of Jesus. The demon that had caused her to check out was overshadowing her soul-man and not allowing her to function as herself.

In the demonized state, when the spirit takes control, the demonized is in an unconscious state. His personality is eclipsed while the demon personality takes over. <u>The new personality manifests itself in facial expressions, physical manifestations, feelings, and statements that belong to it,</u>

not to the temporarily eclipsed personality of the victim.
(29)   *Underline added by this author*

"At least two of these personalities or personality states recurrently take full control of the person's behavior. (30)

When she dissociated, she would just stare off into space. Then, by calling her by her real name, I would get her to use all her faculties and she would groan, shake her head, and come back. It was awesome watching this going on. Praise God for the power of deliverance!! The devil does not have more power than we believers, when we use the **NAME OF JESUS!!**

I believe this is what Jesus was trying to do with the man in the country of the Gadarenes who had the legion of demons. Jesus was trying to get the man to come into agreement with Him when He asked him his name. The man was overpowered by the demons, and Jesus was trying to call his spirit to attention and get him to use all his faculties in this battle.

When he saw Jesus from afar, he ran and worshiped Him. [7]And he cried out with a loud voice and said, "What have I to do with You, Jesus, Son of the Most High God? I implore You by God that You do not torment me." [8]For He said to him, "Come out of the man, unclean spirit!"

⁹Then He asked him, "<u>What *is* your name</u>?" And he answered, saying, "My name *is* Legion; for we are many."

Mark 5:6-9

Jesus was anointed of the Holy Spirit, and He knows everything, so Jesus did not have to ask the demon what his name was. The demon was so strong in this man that he could not talk; therefore it was the demon talking at this time. Jesus was trying to help the man to help himself.

The Sunday after her deliverance, I was preaching in the church in Illinois where L_____ received Jesus. After the service she told me that was the first time she had ever remembered the whole service. She had always "checked out" and would not realize how long a service was. She said it was real long, but the funny thing about it was that I had purposely made it a shorter sermon, because I was real tired from everything we had done with her. The exciting thing is the fact she was able to stay connected through an entire church service without the demonic mind-programming causing her to dissociate.

Now I will share some of L_____'s testimony; quotes from letters she wrote over the course of the year after her deliverance.

"Most things have been going real well and other things are pretty lousy. Halloween wasn't the greatest, but it sure was better than the years before."

"I want to express my gratitude to you for helping me. I don't think I can totally put in writing how much the time you've spent with me has meant and helped me."

"Everyday with Jesus is better than the day before. How else can I say that everything is great, not perfect, but it is great."

"I sleep just about every night through <u>without</u> nightmares."

"The thing that makes me rejoice the most, is when I can remember an entire day, they seem so long sometimes."

"I got my driver's license. I'm not sure if I told you already but my family told me that I would never drive; but the curse has been broken and I've got my driver's license!"

"I'm finding myself getting stronger in the Lord and whose I am, instead of the things I've done."

"I wish you could have known me more and seen how much I've changed in the past year and especially since September."

Since it was her parents who committed the terrible atrocities against her and they were still in the coven, I recommended that she not associate with them. This meant not talking to them on the phone or having any contact with them at all. She said it was the hardest not to talk to her Grandma, but she realized that it was necessary if she was to maintain her deliverance and healing. The last I heard from her, she was getting married to a fine Christian man and they were moving to Wisconsin.

NOTES: DISSOCIATION AND AMNESIA

27 James G. Friesen, Uncovering the Mystery of MPD ... (San Bernardino: Here's Life Publishers, 1991), 114.

28 Ibid, 115.

29 Merrill F. Unger, What Demons Can Do To Saints (Chicago: Moody Press, 1991), 143.

30 The American Psychiatric Association: Diagnostic and Statistical Manual of Mental Disorders, 3rd ed. (Washington, DC: American Psychiatric Association, 1987), 272.

UNEQUALLY YOKED WITH UNBELIEVERS

◧ — ◨

I have heard of a practice or type of ministry that teaches, "*You need to lead all the alter personalities to the Lord and get them saved, because they cannot come together and be integrated with other personalities that are unbelievers.*" They base this practice on this scripture:

Do not be unequally yoked together with unbelievers. For what fellowship has righteousness with lawlessness? And what communion has light with darkness?
2 Corinthians 6:14

This is an improper interpretation of this scripture. This scripture is referring to Christians becoming entangled and attached to non-Christians, such as in marriage, business, and other partnerships.

When you accepted Jesus Christ as your savoir, your spirit-man was saved. Jesus came to sit upon the mercy seat in your Holy of

Holies. Salvation is a spiritual event, not a soulish one. Your spirit was saved and became born-again, not your soul – mind, will, and emotions - which is your personality:

"Personality traits are enduring patterns of perceiving, relating to, and thinking about the environment and oneself, and are exhibited in a wide range of important social and personal contexts." (31)

These are characteristics of our soul – personality - that become renewed through discipline, bible study, deliverance, and even counseling sometimes; but that is a process. Remember I said that the born-again experience was the event when your spirit is born again; the process is the salvation of your soul. According to Romans 12, our soul is renewed by the Word of God: *"Be not conformed to the patterns of this world."* In other words, do not be conformed to the patterns of the world when dealing with this. *"Be transformed by the renewing of your mind".* Now, let's call this as it is - demonic!! If a different voice is manifesting out of a person and if the therapist says, *"Now that's an alter personality. I've got to get that alter personality to accept Jesus, so it can integrate with one who has already accepted Jesus, otherwise they would be unequally yoked"*, they are trying to get a demonic personality to accept Jesus. They cannot do so; they have a place already prepared for them, and it is not heaven.

Jesus said in John 3:6, *"That which is born of the flesh is flesh, and that which is born of the Spirit is spirit."* When we were first born, we were born in the flesh as a little baby - flesh gives birth to flesh. When we were born-again, our spirit was birthed of God. God is Spirit and He gives life to our spirit.

But as many as received Him, to them He gave the <u>right to become children of God,</u> to those who believe in His name: <u>13who were born</u>, not of blood, nor of the will of the flesh, nor of the will of man, but <u>of God</u>.
John 1:12-13

And if Christ *is* in you, the body *is* dead because of sin, <u>but the Spirit *is* life because of righteousness</u>.
Romans 8:10

Our personality is a part of our soul-man, which will be renewed. It is not spirit, and therefore, it cannot be born-again! Since it is our spirit that is born again, and not our soul, how can you lead alter personalities to the Lord? You can't do it. Remember, they are all liars and you cannot trust them. I have read material that says the demons must tell the truth when you bind them and command them to speak only the truth. Then when you speak to the voices and lead them in a prayer of repentance and salvation, it must be an "alter" because demons will not confess Jesus as Lord. Have you ever asked a person if they knew Jesus and then led them in a sinner's prayer to be born-again? Did you ever think that they may have just been saying the words to get what they wanted or to get rid of you? Demons will do the same thing and will lie and say words that you want to hear, but they cannot be born-again!! Like I always say, *"How can you get a demon saved?"* They had their time with God, as angels, but because of their rebellion and subsequent expulsion from Heaven, they are doomed to the fires of hell.

Then He will also say to those on the left hand, 'Depart from Me, you cursed, into the everlasting fire <u>prepared for the devil and his angels</u>:

Matthew 25:41

Now let's go back to this issue of dissociation. At a point during abuse and/or a traumatic event, a person will give up because of the fear and hopelessness and then allow a strongman to enter and develop "demonic personalities." One "demonic personality" will go by one name and others will have their own names. In **Figure 4 (page 81)**, I made them different heights because some may manifest as a child and others as adults. They will even sound like different genders and different ages. The real person has been hiding for so long that their personality does not manifest. The demonic personalities may be the major manifestation, but they are not supposed to be there. I call them "illegal souls" because in James 1:8 it speaks of a "double-minded" man. The Greek for that word is "dipsuchos", which means "two-souled". You have one soul, but they are there illegally. Those demons will tell the real person, "You had better get away from that minister," (one walking in the authority of the name of Jesus). To the demons, the person walking in this authority is the "Big Bad Wolf." The demons will tell the real person, *"You better not go see him. You had better get away from him. They are going to hurt you. If we leave and are all gone, you will be a nothing, a big zero. How will you ever survive?"* When the abuse begins at a very young age in their life and they have not had the opportunity to develop emotionally, sometimes they will believe this, and it is very hard for the real person to trust enough to come out. That first dissociation, or checking out, will usually occur when they are very young (even as a baby sometimes); they leave (hide) and go to that "safe place" and never really develop emotionally. To someone who has never truly developed emotionally, the thought of going out into a world of grown-ups is very scary. Every time the person checked out, a demon came in. Think of this process as when the fear and hopelessness came in, Phillip shut down and something else took over his soulish emotions, will and mind. It is basically the same thing as being hypnotized. If you are hypnotized, you have no control over your soul and someone else has the authority. If you experience trauma involving you or your family members or others, you may checkout - dissociate - and stay at that age in your soul - mind, will, and emotions. Sometimes when this person comes back, they are in another world and they do not understand what is happening. When they come back, they may be twenty-five years old chronologically, but emotionally they are still three years old. The demons are talking to a three year old. The demons will speak to the three year old and say things like: *"You had better get out of here because if we all leave, you won't be able to make it. You will die. You do not know how to do all the things that are required of an adult. We are your friends. They are trying to hurt you."* Now saying this to a three year old will have some effects. That is why the world will tell you that MPDs are afraid to come out. It is because all these demons are talking to this little child and saying, *"You will die. You'll never make it. If I leave, you're not going to make it."* There is tremendous fear. The demons will try to convince the child that the person ministering in the authority of the Name of Jesus is an enemy.

One needs to acknowledge the fact that an MPD is not really manipulative, although it looks that way. The real person is just afraid. They have been doing this for so long that the demons will be manipulative and very destructive toward others. Some therapists will tell the MPD that when those thoughts come, just tell them to be quiet. I say, *"Hallelujah. That's what the Bible says – `take captive every thought'."*

> **casting down arguments and every high thing that exalts itself against the knowledge of God, <u>bringing every thought into captivity</u> to the obedience of Christ, ...**
>
> 2 Corinthians 10:5

But the world says, "You tell those thoughts to be quiet until you get back to see me." The therapist becomes the savior. That's why I tell people all the time, *"I'm not your savior. I may fail you. Jesus is your deliverer, and I am just a vessel He is using."* But in the world the therapist becomes the savior. He talks to the alter personalities. He will have the person logging and journaling events and reactions and telling what goes on.

The world will say that an MPD will self-destruct and leave therapy if you begin to reveal too much. Actually, demons are being exposed and they run. I have had people who are scheduled for an appointment come to me and tell me, *"This has been the worst week of my life. I was coming down the road and the voices were telling me, 'You don't have to go see Phillip Morris'."* The person begins to remember, and the demons cause them to run because they don't want to be exposed. That is one reason why an MPD will run from therapist to therapist. At other times, the therapist will realize that he cannot help this person and will refer them; then they start all over with someone new. Another reason is, even if psychiatry and therapists do manage to help some, it takes so long that the client may become frustrated and leave on their own.

When the three year old was going through the abuse and the fear and the hopelessness came in, the three year old checked out. The demons told him that they would protect and/or comfort him. They will say, "This is a "safe place" and you are safe here." So he went to what he thought was a "safe place", and the demonic personality was beginning to be formed. Then whenever there is a subsequent stressful situation, the three year old will check out and go to the supposedly "safe place". These demonic personalities get stronger and the three year old gets weaker. Then the familiarity of the demons becomes the safety. It's a whole lot easier for the three year old to go hide and do nothing and just let the demons run everything. That is how the demons can develop a system and run that person's life.

> **The alter named Henry liked going to the library to read poetry; some alters spent hours on the phone; Lauren did lots of aerobics; Trixi took walks; and Big Beth Smith, the host, had no idea where the time went. She *did* know when it was almost time for her husband to get home from work, so she could get something together for dinner. That was her job, and although she did not know about the rest of the system, she did her job well. Fortunately for her, <u>the system worked well enough to get her home by the time her husband got off work</u>. (32)**

One or more of the personalities may function with a reasonable degree of adaptation (e.g. be gainfully employed) while alternating with another personality that is clearly dysfunctional or appears to have a specific mental disorder. (33)

Sometimes an MPD has trouble functioning in the world – keep a job, run a family, etc. One person came to me who had several nests, and they had a system and agreement worked out (**See Figure 8**). The bad ones would not manifest on the job so she could keep her job and make a living. She had a job that required her to be dependable, think and make decisions; and she was good at her job. But once she got home from work, the demons took over and chaos ensued. Her home was a total wreck; she never opened the blinds, and she never allowed anyone to come over. After her deliverance and emotional healing, one of her most thrilling moments was being able to clean her house and have friends over for dinner!

In this woman's childhood, there had been incestuous molestation involving her father and brothers, two cousins and an uncle. Her mother and father both rejected her, and they were abusive to each other also. She suffered physical abuse (slapping, hair pulling, bruising), mental abuse (shamed continually), verbal abuse (called degrading names), and sexual abuse. The sexual abuse began when she was one year old and continued until she was almost nine. She had thoughts of suicide, had been in a mental institution, and hypnotized. She had many recurring nightmares, and her most specific fear was being able to trust anyone.

She was a born-again Christian who had been water baptized, Holy Spirit baptized, spoke in tongues and was attending a charismatic Christian church. She was hindered in: her prayer life, praise and worship, Bible study, moving in the gifts of the Spirit, operating in the fruit of the Spirit, and hearing God's voice. She went to her church for help and received counseling, but there was no improvement in her life; she felt abandoned and not understood by her counselors at church. I knew her pastors, and they are wonderful people of God with a tremendous pastoral anointing upon them. But they did not understand what they were dealing with, and it hurt her. She came to me when a friend told her about me and after she discussed it with her pastors.

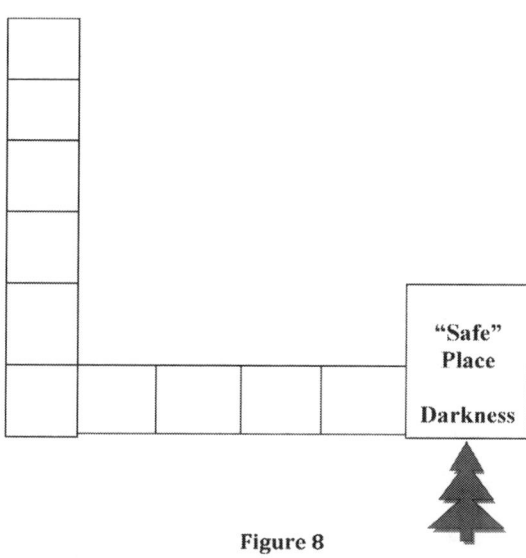

Figure 8

While working with her, the Lord revealed to me this layout of her personality (**see Figure 8**). I had never seen anything like this, but each demonic personality had a room where it stayed. It looked like a motel. Her real personality (herself) was in the last room, which had two stories. I had to deal with each demonic personality individually and work through the fear associated with each one. When one would be bound and successfully cast out, I would then spiritually "blow up" the "room" in which it lived. Every time we would begin work, she would see herself in her room ("Safe" Place), playing with little "children", and there was always a "dark figure" standing in one corner in front of the door. She was told that the "dark figure" was the Holy Spirit standing there to protect her, while she played with her "friends".

While working with her, I would bind all demons and forbid them to operate, but the Lord led us to work with only one at a time. This was for her protection and to allow her to assimilate the information slowly. This is in line with scriptures in both the Old & New Testaments concerning the Lord driving out our enemies. God is protective of us and will not do anything that we are not ready to walk in. He wants us to grow strong enough (increase) in Him to be able to rule in our own house (soul & body).

I will not drive them out from before you in one year, lest the land become desolate and the beast of the field become too numerous for you. [30]Little by little I will drive them

out from before you, until you have increased, and **you inherit the land**.

Exodus 23:29-30

"When an unclean spirit goes out of a man, he goes through dry places, seeking rest, and finds none. ⁴⁴Then he says, 'I will return to my house from which I came.' And when he comes, he finds *it* empty, swept, and put in order. ⁴⁵Then he goes and takes with him seven other spirits more wicked than himself, and they enter and dwell there; and the last *state* of that man is worse than the first. So shall it also be with this wicked generation."

Matthew 12:43-45

The key word in this scripture is "**EMPTY**". One needs to study the Word of God to increase and occupy the house (our soul); then the enemy cannot come in to re-occupy the house. Remember, one with this problem must be able to trust her minister and the people in her support system.

After approximately six weeks, we were working with her in her "room" and during prayer, the "dark figure" moved just a little bit to one side and she saw outside the room. She was amazed because it was light outside and there was a tree just outside the door. And there were real children having fun playing in the light, then she realized that what she was led to believe were her "friends" were really just demons, and the "dark figure" was a strongman that was keeping her in bondage. He was not a "Protector", but the "Strongman" that was orchestrating her captivity. Once his true identity was revealed, she had no more fear of him. Then she fell out of agreement with the lies she had believed, and we were able to cast him out. Then we began to work on the other areas of her life. She would come to me with a memory from her childhood, and we would deal with it to bring deliverance and healing. Because of the terrible memories of pain and unkempt appearance, she suffered with Obsessive Compulsive Disorder in her personal dress. She was always clean in her appearance, but her home was a wreck because the demons controlled the house.

She suffered with shame and trust issues, which produced anger and disappointment. After almost two months, she said she was starting to get in touch with real feelings as a whole person and not disassociated. In one session I shared the truth about getting her soul and spirit in agreement concerning how God sees her. The next week when she returned, she looked great and said she had a great week. She got a revelation of God as her father and her identity through Him and that He has given her everything she needs. After four months, she was delivered and in her right mind concerning the incest and was ready to move on to other events.

Up to now, everyone knew her by a shortened form of her real name. I explained to her about an "illegal soul" and she agreed to fall out of agreement with it, bind it, cast it out, and go by her real name.

This short name was a tie to the abuse and allowed that demon access to her thoughts. After that, she had some separation and vulnerability issues that we dealt with and now she was feeling good about herself; she was even cleaning her house and keeping it maintained! The period of her life when she was "Little _____", had troubled her, but when we prayed and released "Little _____", she could now see that it was a continuum of her life. She could now see a good girl and accept herself at that age. This was after six months of sessions. I continued to work with her for a little over a year; and last I heard, she is still at her church and serving God and doing fine.

But let us return to the "Safe Place" issue; it is really not safe, just familiar, because the memories are filled with familiar spirits. So whenever trauma or pressure comes, the three year old checks out and the familiarity takes over. The familiarity seems like safety, but you need to tell them that where they are going and what is happening is not safe, it is just familiar. These are familiar spirits and demonic; they are not your friends. All their life the person has checked out; the demon has taken over; and they just sit back and play as a little child. They feel nothing, and they have no thoughts about the present; the demons are running the show. Whenever they get into a stressful situation, they think of the demons as their friends, because it seems they (the demons) rescue them and handle the situation. When the opportunity for deliverance arrives, then the thoughts come, *"I don't want to lose my friends. I won't know what to do."* During deliverance, I tell the person that it is not their friend;

it is a demon, a familiar spirit. Also, that this is not a "safe place", just familiar. Their spirit-man is the real person, and he goes by the given name. I tell them to rise up and fight this from the inside. I call them by their given name and tell them to come into agreement with me and fall out of agreement with the demons. (I believe Jesus did this with the Gadarenes demoniac in Mark 5). I keep telling them during the deliverance, *"This is not a friend, it is a familiar spirit. You are just used to it being there. You will not die if they leave. You are God's child, made in the image of God. Rise up in Jesus' name and tell these demons to go."*

NOTES: UNEQUALLY YOKED WITH UNBELIEVERS

31 The American Psychiatric Association: Diagnostic and Statistical Manual of Mental Disorders, 3rd ed. (Washington, DC: American Psychiatric Association, 1987), 335.

32 James G. Friesen, Uncovering the Mystery of MPD: Its Shocking Origins ... Its Surprising Cure (San Bernardino: Here's Life Publishers, 1991), 113.

33 (The American Psychiatric Association), 270.

SUPPORT SYSTEMS

People that you are working with need to know that you are there for them and they are precious and important. They need to have something solid to hang onto when they start to come out of hiding. It is best, and really important, if family, as long as they are not the abusers, can be there to support and help them through this time.

> **It was important for me to have a session with Beth's husband and to explain as much as possible about her condition. I already knew him pretty well, and he accepted the diagnosis fully. He was remarkably supportive and understanding. … …. <u>It would be inaccurate to talk about Beth's progress without highlighting her husband's contribution</u>. He helped her immeasurably and she was headed for quick progress because of it. (34)**

Multiple Personality Disorder, Psychological or Demonic?

The family probably has already gone through hell and is extremely frustrated, especially if the person has never been diagnosed properly. But remember, the struggle is not with that person, it is against the demons that are causing the problem. If that person is serious and wants help, they can get help.

> **Finally, my brethren, be strong in the Lord and in the power of His might. ¹¹Put on the whole armor of God, that you may be able to stand against the wiles of the devil. ¹²For we do not wrestle against flesh and blood, but against principalities, against powers, against the rulers of the darkness of this age, against spiritual** *hosts* **of wickedness in the heavenly** *places.*
>
> **Ephesians 6:10-12**

> **For though we walk in the flesh, we do not war according to the flesh. ⁴For the weapons of our warfare** *are* **not carnal but mighty in God for pulling down strongholds, ⁵casting down arguments and every high thing that exalts itself against the knowledge of God, bringing every thought into captivity to the obedience of Christ,**
>
> **2 Corinthians 10:3-5**

I attended a seminar in which Dr. Friesen said there are different personalities and some may have a demon. But that demon will hide behind that personality, so you may have to call out the personality and talk to it in order to get to the demon. He believes that a "divided" person must turn over every part of their personality to Jesus. Here are some quotes to explain this.

> **Here is the way an exorcism session proceeded in Rosie's MPD/SRA therapy. We were doing some "house" imagery, and the new alter that we had met in the conference room was in a lot of torment. Although Rosie had evil spirits delivered from her at different times previously, this alter turned out to be a demonic point of attachment that had resisted previous expulsions – a satanic stronghold. The demons were able to use the divisions of her heart, including the parts that were occluded by amnesia, to maintain their attachment. They could keep hiding from the "Christian" alters, and thereby avoid being directly exorcised. Now that the demonized alter had been uncovered, we were able to go ahead with the exorcism. (35)**

Dr. Friesen believes that different personalities may have "sequestered spirits".

> **Here is how I have seen that concept at work in MPD clients. In order for people to be free of oppression, they must have faith and trust in God, and they must**

be willing to turn over every part of their lives to Him. That would seem a straightforward experience for most people. A simple prayer and a heartfelt desire to be His follower in every aspect of life is all it takes. But when many personalities share the same body, things are quite a bit more complicated – turning over every part of the life is impossible because the different parts don't know each other! (36)

Remember folks; these are demons, not human personalities. I do not talk to demons. Jesus told them to be quiet and do not speak. He is our example, and He said if we believe, we will do the same things He did. I believe, and therefore I do it like He did.

Sometimes, during dissociation the person will build a wall around their emotions and feelings because of the fear and hopelessness. They feel like they are safe behind that wall, so whenever a pressure situation arises, they checkout and hide behind it. The problem with walls is the denial associated with them. The person thinks they are being protected from a bad situation, but they are only alienating themselves from the outside world. They think they are keeping the evil out, but do not realize they are also blocking the healing from God. A memory is like a container that holds information of our past. If it was traumatic and we "checked out" or dissociated, then we will develop walls to keep that hidden.

In the diagram below, I point out the difference between open memories and closed, or walled, memories. The double arrows represent areas where we had two-way "safe" communication of information in life that we can remember.

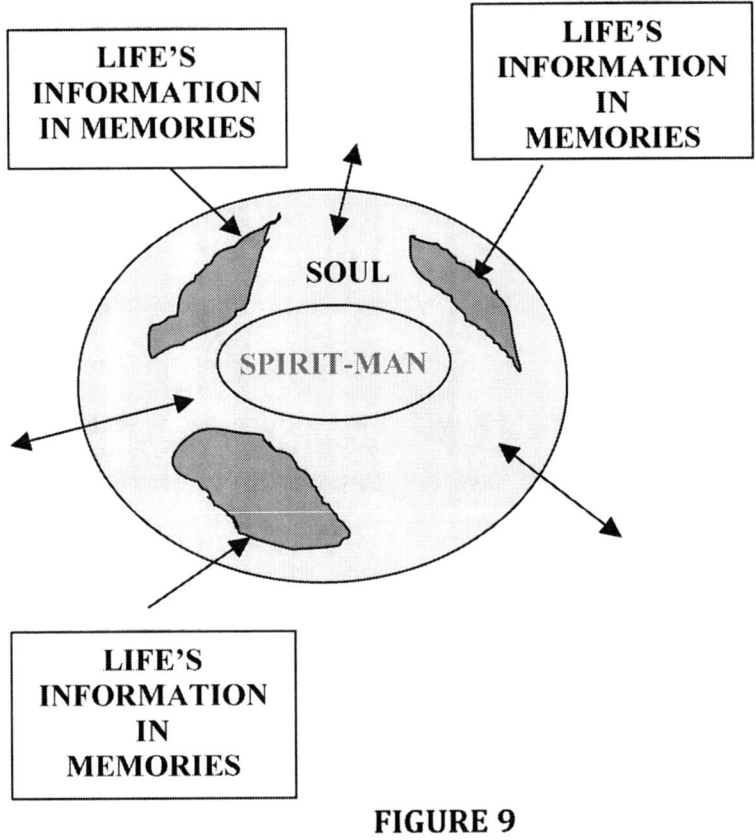

FIGURE 9

The shaded areas represent the memories that we have allowed walls to be built around. In a person with total amnesia, they are the traumatic events that are not remembered. These become strongholds in the person's life that must be pulled down and destroyed with Divine powered weapons, not humanistic theories of psychiatry through years of talking. Secular psychiatry would say that the gray areas are separate personalities that need to be integrated into the host personality. But, we must deal with these things in the spiritual realm to be truly successful.

> **For though we walk in the flesh, we do not war according to the flesh. ⁴For <u>the weapons of our warfare *are* not carnal but mighty in God for pulling down strongholds,</u> ⁵casting down arguments and every high thing that exalts itself against the knowledge of God, bringing every thought into captivity to the obedience of Christ,**
>
> **2 Corinthians 10:3-5**

Eventually you will have to tear down that wall. But first, they need to be assured that someone will be there to love and help them. That's where family is really important, whether it is physical or church family.

I worked with a lady who was a registered nurse until age 30, at which time she began to have memory flashbacks from childhood satanic ritual abuse. At first they were just dreams at night, then, she began having memories during the day. She thought she was losing her mind. She came to me when she was 33 years old. For a year and a half she had been in and out of different psych hospitals, and her husband's insurance had paid out over $500,000.00 on her treatments! She first was diagnosed with Depression, then Post Traumatic Stress Disorder, and finally as MPD in 1993. Her sexual abuse began when she was an infant of less than one year old by her father on his visitation weekends, (her mother and father were divorced already), then other family members also. Then she was taken into the satanic cult to which her biological birth father and other members of his family (her uncles, grandfather, and others) belonged. Other members of the cult included a Chief of Police and a preacher of an Assembly of God church – he was the cult leader! There were people from several ethnic groups – Caucasian, Negro, and Mexican – some legal and some illegal.

She experienced ritualistic trauma such as: a rabbit was killed, the blood was poured on her, and she was made to drink some of the blood. One time a Hispanic lady and she were tortured. They killed the Hispanic lady, but she was hung on a cross. Then they took her down from the cross and made her decide which of two babies would be killed, while she was forced to hold onto the knife. Because of the trauma of abuse, she became very good at dissociation. She continued to dissociate until the fourth grade.

I met her at a deliverance conference I was hosting at our church. When she came in, I was teaching on "Illegal Souls" and "Multiple Personality Disorder". After just a few minutes, she became very terrified, ran into the restroom, and hid under the sink. My wife went into the restroom and had to literally pray her out from under the sink. She came out and sat through the rest of my teaching, but

Multiple Personality Disorder, Psychological or Demonic?

she was terrified and cringing all the time. It was not her that was afraid of what I was saying; it was the demons in her that were afraid of being exposed. Her mother and stepfather had brought her to the conference, so afterwards we talked and scheduled a session for the next week. We began working with her in the last week of September. I was seeing her three days a week, and she was progressing well, but Halloween was a terrible setback. When she saw the paper ghosts and goblins hanging from trees in people's yards, she freaked out! It was so bad that her husband had to take her to the hospital for anxiety attacks. I went to the hospital and ministered to her in the ICU; she received a lot of deliverance and freedom and was able to go home the next day. The next week it was revealed that she had been the queen of the coven and there was a Protector Spirit in her that was the Strongman. So I had her break and renounce all inward agreements, covenants, vows, and mental assents with the Protector Spirit and commanded it to leave her. It left and she had a major breakthrough! I continued to work with her for over a year. The next Halloween when she began to get stressed about all the decorations, she called me; I prayed with her on the phone and she was fine. The year after that, she had no problems at all.

She had body memories (demons manifesting) in her body, especially around, and in, her vaginal area. We had her break all ungodly soulties with family members and other members of the coven. We also had her renounce and bind the illegal soul with the name that the coven had given her and cast it out.

Also we did the same with all the fantasy playmates she had as a child. She renounced all blood sacrifices and covenants that she had participated in with the coven. Then we bound all the demonic spirits that came in through those and commanded them to leave her.

When she would come for an appointment, she would tell me what she was struggling with that week, and we would begin to pray and ask God to help us. We prayed for discernment and asked Jesus to help us along the way. Only Jesus knows all the truth, and when He exposes it, He does it in a way that heals and does not frighten or hurt.

And you shall know the truth, and the truth shall make you free." **John 8:32**

She was the first SRA survivor that I had worked with, and I was taught by the Lord as I went along. During the process, when she was at home and would experience trouble, she would immediately call me. This happened quite often at all times of the day or night (demons do not care what time it is when they manifest). I told her and her husband that it was okay to call me at any time (she was the reason I bought my first cell phone), but before they called me, I wanted **him** to pray for her and forbid all demons to manifest, then call me if things did not get better. Her deliverance progressed much more rapidly when he became involved. I believe it was because she felt loved and supported at home by her own family. She had been in psych hospitals and therapy and therefore separated from them off and on for a year and a half! After just three months of outpatient therapy, she was back home functioning as a wife and mother. Her step-dad says I am the best demon chaser in the world. She is fine now and working as a research nurse for a major hospital organization.

I have worked with people who have been set free and then went back into bad situations at home, and they slip right back into it. If they don't have a support system, they become afraid, rebuild their wall, and allow the demons back in. So, it is real important that the person knows they have a support system. When I am working with someone like this, I make sure they have a church home. Sometimes I will call the home pastor and talk with him. Remember the girl that got lost on the way home (*by the way, she did make it home and has no more problems like that*), she has her own pastor who is very supportive in all this. Plus she has another friend who is a pastor's wife and very supportive. Support systems are real important. But, I am talking about a support **system,** not a **support group** that continually rehashes all the past.

> **Finally, brethren, whatever things are true, whatever things *are* noble, whatever things *are* just, whatever things *are* pure, whatever things *are* lovely, whatever things *are* of good report, if *there is* any virtue and if *there is* anything praiseworthy—meditate on these things.**
>
> **Philippians 4:8**

We need to keep our eyes on Jesus, not on the past and its' abuses!!

NOTES: SUPPORT SYSTEMS

34 James G. Friesen, Uncovering the Mystery of MPD ... (San Bernardino: Here's Life Publishers, 1991), 45.

35 Ibid, 262-263.

36 Ibid, 238.

INTEGRATION

Psychology says that you need to integrate all these personalities. Integration means to bring them together into one, to use the strengths of each one to work for the good of the person. That is why some ministries say you have to get all the personalities saved so they can all join together and not be unequally yoked. Personality is a part of our soul – mind, will, and emotions; our spirit is saved, not our soul. Salvation is of a spiritual nature, not an intellectual one. Our soul is renewed with the Word of God, a discipleship process that takes time. Salvation is a supernatural spontaneous miracle where our human spirit is born-again by the Spirit of God. One needs to remember demons cannot be saved!

> **But as many as received Him, to them He gave the right to become children of God, to those who believe in His name: <u>13who were born</u>, not of blood, nor of the will of the flesh, nor of the will of man, but <u>of God</u>.**
>
> **John 1:12-13**

God created man and He gave us a sound mind.

"For God has not given us a spirit of fear, but of power and of love and of a <u>sound mind</u>."   **2 Timothy 1:7**

Before a person comes in for a deliverance session, we have a questionnaire for them to fill out. One of the questions is: *"Did you have any imaginary playmates as a child?" "If `Yes', name them."* One lady answered *"Yes"*, and wrote two names down. When she came in for her session, I was sitting in as an overseer, training others. As they were asking her some preliminary questions, I asked Doug, the minister, *"Have you asked her about those two names on there?"* He said, *"No, I was just getting ready to do that."* This lady was a 33-year old, sound, rational woman sitting very calm and composed. Then he said, *"You have in your questionnaire the names of two imaginary playmates,"* and then mentioned the names. **<u>Immediately</u>**, this woman who was sitting there just as calm as could be, threw her arms up over her head as if to fend off attacking blows, and began to plead, *"NO! NO! Please don't beat me mommy! Please don't beat me, mommy! Please don't beat me mommy! Please mommy - NO!"* Immediately, just like that. Well, Doug looked at me and I said, *"I think we just lost her."* I slowly rolled my office chair over to her and began to work with her. I began to take authority, in the Name of Jesus, over the demons in both nests of the two illegal souls. Basically, I did a group deliverance service in one person.

Two and a half hours later, she was set free and told us; *"I have never felt like this in my life. I feel whole. There's not all that confusion. Before, I may see a cat and one part of me would have the C, another part of me would have the A, and another part of me would have the T. But now I feel whole."* It was awesome! **Two and a half hours**, not years!! She said this was really wonderful because she felt whole for the first time in her life.

If you have been suffering with illegal souls, Jesus loves you and you are important to Him. Almost 2,000 years ago, **Jesus prayed this prayer to our Heavenly Father for you to be integrated and become one in Him:**

> "I pray for them. I do not pray for the world, but for those whom You have given Me, for they are Yours. And all Mine are Yours, and Yours are Mine, and I am glorified in them. Now I am no longer in the world, but these are in the world, and I come to You. Holy Father, keep through Your name those whom You have given me, **that they may be one** as We are. While I was with them in the world, I kept them in Your name. Those whom You gave Me I have kept; and none of them is lost except the son of perdition, that the scriptures might be fulfilled. But now I come to You, and these things I speak in the world, that they may have My joy fulfilled in themselves. I have given them Your word; and the world has hated them

because they are not of the world, just as I am not of the world. I do not pray that You should take them out of the world, but that You should keep them from the evil one. They are not of the world, just as I am not of the world. Sanctify them by Your truth. Your word is truth. As you sent me into the world, I also have sent them into the world. And for their sakes I sanctify Myself, that they also may be sanctified by the truth. I do not pray for these alone, but also for those who will believe in Me through their word; <u>that they all may be one</u>, as You, Father, are in Me, and I in You; <u>that they also may be one in Us</u>, that the world may believe that You sent Me. And the glory which You gave Me I have given them, <u>that they may be one just as We are one: I in them, and You in Me; that they may be made perfect in one</u>, and that the world may know that You have sent Me, and have loved them as You have loved Me."

John 17:9-23

The Word says that we have the mind of Christ. And Jesus said,

"I in them and You in Me. <u>May they be brought to complete unity</u> to let the world know that You sent Me and have loved them even as You have loved Me."

John 17:23 (NIV)

Jesus has provided the way for us to be brought into complete unity, and that is what I prayed for the lady in the above illustration. While praying for her I said, *"Father God, I ask that you answer Jesus' prayer for this lady right now, that she may be brought into complete unity as one."* After the prayer, she said, *"I have never felt this whole in my life. I feel like I'm all together. I'm whole."* It was awesome. Just two and a half hours; now we are operating on God's terms and His timetable! The other exciting part of this is that two weeks later she received her registered nurse certificate and went to work! She has had problems since, because she did not have a support system and she quit coming to see me on her personal sessions. I also have monthly deliverance services, and I recommend that everyone continue coming for a period of time on a regular basis as follow-up. It is real important that you have some support as you walk out this deliverance and continue to "work out your salvation." We can help those who come and do what we ask, but rebellion to authority opens the door to a lot of demons.

Another lady who came to me is very brilliant – bordering on genius – but had some major personality problems, she was multiple. At the time she was going to school working on her Masters degree. Here is her testimony as she wrote it and gave it to me.

"I wanted to share something with you about myself:

Anyway, you know that when we were visiting my grandparents; my grandfather molested me. I was 10; and I told my mom who told my dad and then nothing happened. I remember crying at the kitchen table while they just looked at me; and they never brought it up again. They also left me alone there with him a lot, though nothing ever happened because I wouldn't stay in the room with him. I think he did a lot to her (Mom) growing up so I understand why she couldn't deal with it; but at the time I figured that I was on my own and I could not trust or depend on anyone. I was very angry.

When I got back to school, I was still very angry. My mom basically never talked to me. She was constantly either angry or depressed and Dad never came out of his computer room much. At school, stuff happened too. Too much to go into but for the next 8 years NO ONE talked to me at home or at school in any type of supportive manner. At school, I was that outcast kid and every day I was told to go away, you're stupid, etc. You know how kids are. I tried to get my parents to let me go to another school. They wouldn't even acknowledge AGAIN that there was any problem. So I lived in fear at school and at home.

My parents are fine now; but then they constantly talked about how they hated their parents and their families; while they told them to their face they loved them. My dad told my mom he loved her, but then when he hugged her he would look at me and roll his eyes. What is that supposed to mean? Whenever I was around Mom would get upset; which would get Dad upset. Dad constantly told me I was stupid, and he used big words to prove it. My brother pushed me through a plate glass window once; and also chased me around the kitchen table with a knife. Sooner or later I figured out nowhere was safe, no one really loved me, and I must be a really bad person and SURELY this was all my fault.

I retreated into a different personality and chose to be someone else, but the anger and hurt was still there. I have had a horrible attitude for a long time, out of anger, hurt, betrayal and fear. I remember one time watching a show about a family where the girl was upset about something and the dad followed her out of the room to talk to her and make sure she was okay. I saw this when I was 27. I remember being shocked, extremely angry, and sad; I was thinking "Dad's do that? They talk to their kids? They are supposed to help you?" I had no idea!!!

I have tried all my life to prove wrong that little voice that told me I was broken, damaged, irreparable, and it was my fault. My temper and bad behavior only proved to me that it was right; so I tried harder and failed miserably. God brought me to Restoration House Church at a time when I was ready to kill myself because I couldn't take it anymore. I didn't even know what was real and who I was and why I was even here anymore. He slowly started setting me free from things, but it was never what I wanted to change; which was the way I felt about myself, the fear, and the darned attitude. I could not control it and it made me feel so damaged. I kept apologizing to God for making Him look bad and basically for just existing. Yes, things changed, but I was still failing.

In the last month, things have changed. Core things have changed. God has BEGUN a very basic shift in my thinking and beliefs. I KNOW I am okay. It was not, and is not, my fault. I can truly say now that I have feelings, I never felt anything but anger, fear, and sadness before. I can say for a fact that I feel joy, love, and compassion more deeply than I knew you could. I am learning to be who I am, who God made me to be and what that means. I am learning what it means that God is my friend and my father and that he LOVES me and that love is not bad or a synonym or code word for hate. It is really hard to describe where I am right now, but it is a very new place. Somewhat scary as I do not know the landscape yet, nor the new rules or lack of old ones. I am not a shattered vase just glued together that he has to make excuses for, but a new creation that is whole, one that was never broken.

The strange part is what Paul talks about when he talks about the sin nature; that it is still there. But it is not me, nor who I am. It pops up now and then, sometimes I beat it down; sometimes I embrace it and truly regret it and despise myself later. But I get over it and learn from the experience and move on.

When you are learning to speak and step out; you make mistakes. People need to understand and let you learn and grow. I am going to make mistakes. I am often misunderstood. My tone can be blunt and direct and this is often mistaken for aggressiveness, or a challenge. I have never meant any of those things and it is so painful to be wrongfully accused and not believed. I am trying to

change my negative behaviors and I thought I had slipped and inadvertently insulted you by my tone or sharpness.

I am going to be myself, and most people find me intimidating. I have had countless people stop being my friend because I am "too smart". Excuse me, but what is that supposed to mean? Is that my fault? Am I supposed to act dumb? I can't; and I don't think I am that smart, I feel very unsmart and would like to learn a whole lot more about a whole lot more things before I die. I know that I am a really good person with a lot to give, I am very loyal and I would do ANYTHING for my friends, ask Maribel, I mean ANYTHING. Pastor and Maribel are my family; I love my church because it is through their patience and steadfast love of me that I was able to allow God to heal me. I ask that you have patience with me as well for all the reasons above. <u>I am going to make it</u> too."

It took longer with this lady because she would not open up and trust God to heal her. When she was a teenager, she accepted Jesus Christ as her Lord and Savior and was very excited about church and the things she was learning there. But then her mom refused to allow her to attend church, and she believed that God would not protect her. She continued to believe this lie and thought she had to fix her problems herself. The problem was that she was continually failing, which reinforced the lie that God would not protect or deliver her from her troubles. She had difficulty with intimacy because of all the turmoil in her life with the people with whom she should have been able to be intimate. One Father's day I was preaching on the father's role of love, protection, and authority in the home. I said that as a pastor, I was the father-figure in the church; and she got up to leave. She said, "I had one of those and it was not good and I don't need another." My wife had to hold onto her arm to keep her from leaving, but we prayed with her and she has been here for fourteen years now. We love her, and I tell everyone she is like an adopted daughter to me; she thinks of me as her other dad.

When this lady first came to me, she was so distraught that she wanted to quit graduate school. She said it was not her that was learning, and she would not be able to remember any of what she had learned. She was afraid that when she was no longer multiple, but healed and "in her right mind", she would not remember anything. I assured her that everything was going into her memory bank and when she needed it, it would be there. Now she has a managerial position in a major hospital and is making over $60,000.00 a year! Praise God for His healing miracles.

TREATMENT MODALITIES

Treatment of a multiple personality requires great discernment and patience. When I am in a session with a client, I must be ready to employ a number of different styles and address several areas in the person's life. I have a twenty-three page questionnaire that each client fills out before personal ministry. That is how I find out the personal history and discover other areas of interest to talk about on the client's first visit. In this chapter I will explain the areas to address during deliverance ministry.

Keys of the Kingdom

First I must explain the method of dealing with the demons that are in a person's mind. Jesus has given us the "keys to the kingdom of heaven" to confront demonic powers. These keys of the kingdom are "binding and loosing", which we are able to use through the authority of His name and the power of the Holy Spirit baptism.

> **And I will give you the <u>keys of the kingdom of heaven</u>, and whatever you <u>bind</u> on earth will be <u>bound</u> in heaven, and whatever you <u>loose</u> on earth will be <u>loosed</u> in heaven."**
>
> **Matthew 16:19**

The concept of binding and loosing is a matter of what we allow in our lives. We are the gatekeeper of our life, and we are responsible for what we do or don't do. We are the authority on earth of our own life, and we determine what is lawful, or not, in our life.

TO BIND

> **And I will give you the keys of the kingdom of heaven, and whatever you <u>bind</u> on earth will be bound in heaven, and whatever you loose on earth will be loosed in heaven."**
>
> **Matthew 16:19**

> **Assuredly, I say to you, whatever you <u>bind</u> on earth will be bound in heaven, and whatever you loose on earth will be loosed in heaven.**
>
> **Matthew 18:18**

The transliteration of the Greek word for <u>bind</u> is deo, which is:

#1210: a primary verb; to bind (in various applications, literal or figurative): bind, be in bonds, knit, tie, wind. (37)

by a Chaldean and rabbinical idiom, "to forbid, prohibit, <u>declare to be illicit</u>":

Matthew 16:19; 18:18.   (38)

We have the authority to declare the demons in a person to be illicit, or **unlawful**, because Jesus defeated them by his death, burial, and resurrection.

Having disarmed principalities and powers, He made a public spectacle of them, triumphing over them in it.

Colossians 2:15

[God] disarmed the principalities and powers that were ranged against us and made a bold display and public example of them, in triumphing over them in Him and in it [the cross].   Colossians 2:15 (AMP)

TO LOOSE

The transliteration of the Greek word for <u>loose</u> is luō, which is:

#3089: a primary verb; to "loosen" (literal or figurative): break (up), destroy, dissolve, (un-) loose, melt, put off. (39)

"<u>to declare lawful</u>":   Matthew 16:19; 18:18   (40)

We are to **<u>declare lawful</u>**, or <u>loose</u>, those things that Jesus has already paid the price for and given unto us – every spiritual blessing in the heavenly realms.

> **Blessed be the God and Father of our Lord Jesus Christ, who has <u>blessed us with every spiritual blessing in the heavenly places in Christ,</u>   Ephesians 1:3**

<u>**What can we bind and loose?**</u>

> **I will give you the keys of the kingdom of heaven; <u>and whatever you bind</u> (declare to be improper and unlawful) on <u>earth must be what is already bound in heaven</u>; and whatever <u>you loose</u> (declare lawful) on earth <u>must be what is already loosed in heaven</u>.**
> **   Matthew 16:19 (AMP)**

In order to bind a demon or loose a blessing on earth, it must have already been bound or loosed in heaven. We must use this authority in accordance to God's will and Jesus' accomplished victory. When we use the keys of the kingdom to bind or loose on earth, we are just enforcing what Jesus did before and are continuing to forbid them to operate on the earth.

And I will give you the keys of the kingdom of heaven, and whatever you bind on earth will be bound in heaven, and whatever you loose on earth will be loosed in heaven."
Matthew 16:19

Both verbs – bind (deo) and loose (luo) – used in Matthew 16:19 and 18:18 are perfect passive participles which should have been translated respectively as "having been bound" and "having been loosed" already in the heavens. (41)

The words bind and loose are translated as to indicate continuance in any act or state; equivalent to - <u>shall remain bound</u>, <u>shall remain loosed.</u> When we employ these "keys", we will be victorious as the disciples were:

Then the seventy returned with joy, saying, "Lord, <u>even the demons are subject to us in Your name</u>." Luke 10:17

There are some churches that believe in deliverance and they say they do deliverance. But when someone comes to the altar, they say, "In the name of Jesus, I bind that spirit and command it to come out." They call it casting out demons (and it is), but it does not help someone who is truly suffering from a deeper problem, such as Multiple Personality Disorder. MPD is a more complicated situation and takes more time and work in deliverance, teaching, and counseling. Here are the areas that I address when working with a person.

UNGODLY SOUL TIES

A soul tie is a strong emotional tie with anyone. The problem with soul ties is that soul ties will pull you away from God's plan for your life and you won't be able to fulfill what God has for you. Whenever we love someone so much or have such emotional ties with them, sometimes that can get in the way of being obedient to God because we are swayed by our emotions. That's why you break ungodly soul ties; an ungodly tie will pull you away.

You can have godly and ungodly soul ties with the same people. I have godly soul ties with my son, but if I didn't continually break the ungodly soul ties, I could get pulled into doing something that I shouldn't do because of that emotional tie. Now, I want us to look at some scriptures.

Do not be so deceived *and* misled! Evil companionships (communion, associations) corrupt *and* deprave good manners *and* morals *and* character.

1 Corinthians 15:33 (AMP)

This is what an ungodly soul tie will do. If you hang with the wrong people, you develop soul ties with them and because they're doing it, you'll do it. This scripture is talking about 'guilty by association'.

One can have a strong emotional tie that is not associated with sin or evil, but still be an ungodly connection. When one loves someone so much that all decisions are made based upon feelings, it will hinder them from making sound decisions. The story in Genesis in the Bible of Jacob, Joseph, and Benjamin explains this ungodly type of soul tie. You know the story of Jacob. He had twelve sons. Jacob worked for seven years to get this beautiful wife, got tricked by his father-in-law, and got the ugly sister. I don't know if she was ugly or not (she wasn't as pretty as the other one though), but he worked fourteen years to get two wives. Between the one wife and her maidservant and Rachel's maidservant there were ten children born. Rachel had two children, Joseph and Benjamin. He loved her the most. Obviously, he loved these two sons more than the others.

> **Now Israel loved Joseph more than all his children, because he was the son of his old age. Also he made him a tunic of many colors.** **Genesis 37:3**

Joseph was a dreamer. He is the one for whom his dad made the coat of many colors. Joseph prophesied of things in his life, and his brothers didn't like it; they sold him into slavery, and he went to Egypt. He went to prison, was released, and became second in command in all of Egypt. There's a famine over where Jacob and the other boys live, so he sent the boys off to Egypt to get some food. When they got over there, they didn't recognize Joseph, but he knew who they were. They didn't take Benjamin along, and Joseph asked, "Do you have any other brothers." They said, "We have one other brother, but Dad won't let him out of his sight because his brother was killed, and we can't let anything happen to this boy." So he stays at home. Joseph told them, "Unless you bring everybody over here—unless he comes over—I am not going to give you any food. So they went back and brought him to Egypt. Then Joseph tricks them and slips some gold and stuff in Benjamin's sack. When they leave, he sends his army out and arrests Benjamin for stealing. Reuben, the oldest boy, said, "Well, you don't understand. If we go home and the boy's not with us, our dad will die because his life is bound up in the lad's life."

> **Now therefore, when I come to your servant my father, and the lad is not with us, since <u>his life is bound up in the lad's life</u>, ³¹it will happen, when he sees that the lad is not with us, that he will die. So your servants will bring down the gray hair of your servant our father with sorrow to the grave.** **Genesis 44:30-31**

What I am saying is that Jacob had an ungodly soul tie with Benjamin because he thought Joseph had died. He loved Benjamin so much that if he thought he was dead, Jacob would die. The bad thing was that his life was bound up in the lad's life. There are a whole lot of parents today that have ungodly soul ties with their children or grandchildren, and they cannot make sound decisions concerning them. Whenever Jacob thought that Joseph died, the Bible says Jacob refused to be comforted. "I'll carry this down to my grave with me." This is what happens to people whenever they have such an ungodly soul tie. They refuse to be comforted; they will make wrong decisions. Their thinking is clouded by their emotions.

SEXUAL SOUL TIES

A Christian needs to flee sexual immorality because sexual soul ties are the strongest ones. Whenever you have sex with someone, you become one with them and you sin against the temple of the Holy Spirit. The Bible says that if we defile the temple of the Holy

Spirit, God will destroy us. I believe differently from other people who believe that sin is sin is sin—one sin is the same as the other. I believe that sexual sins are stronger because we are sinning against our own body, which is the temple of the Holy Spirit.

Now it doesn't say if you lie, God will destroy you. But it says if you sin a sexual sin, you sin against your own body - the temple of God; you defile this temple, and He'll destroy you. I know the ties are stronger. I ministered to a young Baptist girl that had ungodly soul ties with a young man. She was in a sexual relationship with him, and she knew it was wrong. He was living with another girl, but would occasionally call her to have sex. She wanted to stop, but every time he called, she could not say no. Whenever we broke the soul ties with him, she was able to say no to him for the first time.

> **Do you not know that you are the temple of God and *that* the Spirit of God dwells in you?** [17] **<u>If anyone defiles the temple of God, God will destroy him</u>. For the temple of God is holy, which *temple* you are.**
>
> 1 Corinthians 3:16-17

> **Or do you not know that he who is joined to a harlot is one body *with her*? For *"the two,"* He says, *"<u>shall become one flesh</u>."* [17] But he who is joined to the Lord is one spirit *with Him*. [18] <u>Flee sexual immorality</u>. Every sin that a man does is outside the body, but <u>he who commits sexual**

immorality sins against his own body. [19] **Or do you not know that your body is the temple of the Holy Spirit** *who is* **in you, whom you have from God, and you are not your own?**   **1 Corinthians 6:16-19**

When I am ministering to someone, I will lead them in a prayer concerning the connection in the spirit realm (soul tie) with every person with whom they have had sexual contact. The Bible says that when we have sex with someone we become one flesh with them (**see scripture above**). This applies to husband and wife also.

Therefore a man shall leave his father and mother and be joined to his wife, and they shall become one flesh.
                                  Genesis 2:24

This can cause trouble in a person's life. When we are soulishly connected to someone else, we may share some of that person's thoughts and desires that are totally contrary to our own. When we experience these other desires or thoughts, we cannot understand where they are coming from, it is from the ungodly soul tie.

If we are one flesh with them, we are connected to them and that needs to be broken. I will have them loose and send back every part of all the people with whom they have had sexual contact. Then I have them call back to them every part of their self from every person with whom they have had sexual contact. At this time I will ask the Lord to restore their soul. I have had many different reactions when I do this, but most say they feel different - more whole.

We can have godly soul ties and ungodly soul ties with people that have hurt us and abused us. It is possible to have godly soul ties and ungodly soul ties with the same people, such as your parents. They provide for your education; they give you clothes; they raise you, but then they might have done something that was bad, at least some things that as a teenager - you thought were bad. Therefore, it put a really bad feeling in you at that time, and it stayed there - it's an ungodly soul tie. Sometimes a member of the family may do things to you that weren't right (touched you in the wrong place or something like that). It might only happen one time; the rest of the time that person was really good. So, everyone in the whole family thinks he/she is a great person, but every time you think of him, that thing he did wrong comes up. That's an ungodly soul tie that needs to be broken. Sometimes people say, "I have forgiven him", but if they do not break the ungodly soul tie, they still have an ungodly connection. So, sometimes it's not a matter of forgiving them because you have already done that and don't want to hold anything bad against them; it's a matter of having an ungodly soul tie.

GODLY SOUL TIES

Now when he had finished speaking to Saul, <u>the soul of Jonathan was knit to the soul of David, and Jonathan</u>

loved him as his own soul. ² **Saul took him that day, and would not let him go home to his father's house anymore.** ³ **Then Jonathan and David made a covenant, because he loved him as his own soul.** ⁴ **And Jonathan took off the robe that** *was* **on him and gave it to David, with his armor, even to his sword and his bow and his belt.   1 Samuel 18:1-4**

King Saul was talking to David just after David killed Goliath. Then Jonathan and David made a covenant because he loved him as his own soul; "And the soul of Jonathan was knit to the soul of David." Jonathan and David had a godly soul tie, and whenever David became king, he wanted to know if there was anybody in Jonathan's family he could do good to. There was only one son left alive - Mephibosheth. David brought him in and gave him back all of Jonathan and Saul's farms and gave him servants to run it, cattle and everything else. And then Mephibosheth ate at the king's table for the rest of his life because he was crippled. That was a godly soul tie between Jonathan and David.

We can have both godly and ungodly soul ties with the same people. A soul tie is a spiritual connection. We need to break the ungodly soul ties and release all parts of those people. The people we have ungodly soul ties with are people we also need to forgive.

UNFORGIVENESS

To forgive means to hold back or not give someone what they deserve. If someone does you wrong, they deserve to be punched in the nose. But you forgive them; you don't give them what they deserve. You hold back; some people have a hard time holding back. They may not punch them in the nose, but they have a hard time holding their tongue. **Forgiveness is a decision; it's not a feeling.** It is an act of your will, and it is not an option if a person wants to walk in freedom. You have to forgive because if you don't, you will not be forgiven. Some people say, "I don't feel like forgiving." I don't care how you feel. It is a decision that you need to make if you want freedom in your life. When we forgive others, we are breaking a hold Satan has on us and allowing them, and us, to be free from restrictions in thought.

Some Reasons To Forgive:

So Satan Doesn't Get An Advantage Over You.

> Now whom you forgive anything, I also *forgive*. For if indeed I have forgiven anything, I have forgiven that one for your sakes in the presence of Christ, [11] **lest Satan should take advantage of us**; for we are not ignorant of his devices.   2 Corinthians 2:10-11

We Forgive So We Can Be Forgiven.

"For if you forgive men their trespasses, your heavenly Father will also forgive you. ¹⁵ But <u>if you do not forgive men their trespasses, neither will your Father forgive your trespasses.</u>   Matthew 6:14-15

There are a whole lot of people that think they are justified in having unforgiveness toward someone else, but they want every one of their own sins to be forgiven. According to God's word, it's not going to happen. If you haven't forgiven others, you cannot be forgiven. You see stories on the news where someone raped and murdered a woman. The family will come out and say, "We forgive them". Everybody says that's just awesome. They do that because they realize what God has said; and they know if they do not forgive, it will destroy their life. That doesn't mean when a family says we forgive them that they just let them go. No. They still go through the trial and the punishment and everything else. But the family forgives because they want to be released from the trauma. If we do not forgive someone from that trauma, we'll be connected to it all the time. It's really interesting that some people say they forgive; then turn around and sue someone. That doesn't really compute with me. If I forgive them and cancel their debt, they don't owe me anything. When you forgive someone you are not letting them off the hook.

Sooner or later they will stand before the righteous Judge Jesus and answer for what they have done.

So It Will Not Hinder Your Gift Being Accepted

> **Therefore if you bring your gift to the altar, and there remember that your brother has something against you, ²⁴ leave your gift there before the altar, and go your way. First be reconciled to your brother, and then come and offer your gift.** **Matthew 5:23-24**

This scripture is really looking at this from the other side. If your brother has something against you, you should take the initiative and go and say, "Please forgive me." We have to forgive others, or we won't be forgiven. But if we have done something wrong and they have unforgiveness toward us, and we don't go and talk to them about it and offer to get it right, then our prayers are being hindered. That's why we have to get unforgiveness out of our life. It doesn't matter whether the other person did something or you did something; it needs to be cleared up and forgiven.

So You Will Not Be Turned Over To The Tormentors.

> **Then Peter came to Him and said, "Lord, how often shall my brother sin against me, and I forgive him? Up**

to seven times?" ²² Jesus said to him, "I do not say to you, up to seven times, but up to seventy times seven.

Matthew 18:21-22

That means unlimited times, however many times he does it. The story goes on to say that the master had a servant who owed him millions of dollars, and he said, "What do I do?" The master went to him and said, "Pay me everything that you owe me." And the guy said, "I don't have it. Please forgive me, and I'll pay you back." The master forgave the man and **cancelled his debt**. That's so important. A lot of times we say we forgive someone, but then we say they still owe me — I forgive them, but now you owe me. No, you haven't forgiven them yet. You need to forgive the person **and cancel the debt**. That's what the master did. He forgave the person and cancelled his debt. If you forgive a person, but then you sue them for something — you still have the problem hanging over you. You have to cancel the debt also to truly be released from unforgiveness. Matthew 18:27 says the master of that servant was moved with compassion, released the person, and forgave him the debt - so there was total forgiveness there. Then that servant went out and found a fellow servant who owed him a few dollars, and he said, "Pay me everything you owe me." He was choking him and demanding, "Give me my money!" And the fellow servant begged, "No. I'm sorry; I don't have it. Will you please forgive me?" The first servant wouldn't do it, and he threw the other one into debtor's prison until he could pay

Multiple Personality Disorder, Psychological or Demonic?

the whole thing. The master found out about it and came back and said to that first one, "You wicked servant. I forgave you all that debt because you begged me. Shouldn't you also have had compassion upon your fellow servant as I have had pity on you?" And his master was angry and delivered him to the torturers until he should pay all that was due to him. And then Jesus said, "**And so my heavenly Father will do to you if each of you from his heart does not forgive his brother his trespasses**." What he's saying there is that if we have unforgiveness toward people and we don't forgive them from our heart, we're going to be tormented. This translation says "and turned him over to the torturers", and King James says "turned him over to the tormentors." Today, that torment is done by demons. If a person has unforgiveness in their heart, it becomes a hindrance to their deliverance. Those demons have permission from God to torment that person according to this scripture in Matthew 18.

They cannot receive deliverance until they do what? **Repent of their unforgiveness and forgive the person.** For what is it that turns God? Repentance. A lot of people do not want to forgive because they feel they are letting this person get by with everything. Whenever you forgive someone, you're not letting him off the hook. You turn them over to Jesus, the righteous judge, to receive their due judgment. Then you're supposed to pray for their salvation and bless them. I don't care what they've done to you; it's not worth hanging on to it.

Multiple Personality Disorder, Psychological or Demonic?

WHO DO WE FORGIVE?

Oppressing Nationalities. Whenever I talk about oppressing nationalities, I mean nationalities that have oppressed your nationality. There was a terrible, terrible blight on this nation called slavery. The blacks have to forgive the whites. The Jews have to forgive the Germans for killing 6 million of them during WWII. The Mexicans have to forgive the Texans for taking their land; Texans have to forget the Alamo and forgive the Mexicans. The Irish and the English—they've been fighting for years. The American Indian must forgive the white man for taking their land. Look at those nationalities that have oppressed the nationalities in your bloodline and forgive them.

Authority Figures – Maybe there are authority figures that have done you wrong, treated you wrong, used you and abused you in various different ways. Those authority figures can be your parents, grandparents, babysitters, teachers, principals, pastors, bosses, all the way up, anybody that's been in authority over you. Those who have abused or hurt you in any way, these are people that you forgive. **You have to forgive God**. Sometimes when something bad happens, some well-meaning people will say, "Well all things work together for good for those who love God." Well if it was a tragedy, it's hard to understand that. Thirty years later they may be able to understand that all things work together for good, but at the moment they have a hard time believing that. They will get mad at

God because they believe it was Him who caused the tragedy. Most people will suppress this anger and unforgiveness because it is not right to be mad at God. Some do not even realize they are angry at God until I lead them in prayer and suddenly they get a release of emotions.

<u>You Have To Forgive Self</u>. Self is a big one. A lot of people are their worst enemy. They haven't forgiven themselves. We all make mistakes somehow, some way, at different times, so we have to forgive ourselves. Sometimes we do something that hurts somebody, they have forgiven us, and it is all cleared up, but we haven't forgiven ourself. And we continue to beat ourselves up and continue to think we are no good and this and that. Therefore what we are doing is breaking the second greatest commandment. The first is to love God with everything, and the second is to love your neighbor as yourself. But if we have unforgiveness towards ourself, how can we love our neighbor? If that's the way you're going to love your neighbor, I praise God I'm not your neighbor because I don't want you loving me like that. If you are hating yourself and thinking bad about yourself, I do not need that type of loving.

<u>SINS OF THE FOREFATHERS</u>

> **And God spoke all these words, saying: ² "I *am* the Lord your God, who brought you out of the land of Egypt, out of the house of bondage. ³ You shall have no other gods**

before Me. ⁴ "You shall not make for yourself a carved image, or any likeness *of anything* that *is* in heaven above, or that *is* in the earth beneath, or that *is* in the water under the earth; ⁵ you shall not bow down to them nor serve them. For I, <u>the Lord your God, *am* a jealous God, visiting the iniquity of the fathers on the children to the third and fourth *generations* of those who hate Me</u>, ⁶ but showing mercy to thousands, to those who love Me and keep My commandments.   Exodus 20:1-6

The sins of your forefathers could be the cause of trouble in your life because they are passed down for three and four generations. We need to confess the sins of our forefathers, and if we do He will remember His covenant with us.

'*But* if they confess their iniquity and the iniquity of their fathers, with their unfaithfulness in which they were unfaithful to Me, and that they also have walked contrary to Me, ⁴¹ and *that* I also have walked contrary to them and have brought them into the land of their enemies; if their uncircumcised hearts are humbled, and they accept their guilt— ⁴² <u>then I will remember My covenant</u> with Jacob, and My covenant with Isaac and My covenant with Abraham I will remember; I will remember the land.   Leviticus 26:40-42

PERSONAL SINS

> Then those of Israelite lineage separated themselves from all foreigners; and <u>they stood and confessed their sins and the iniquities of their fathers</u>. ³ And they stood up in their place and read from the Book of the Law of the Lord their God *for one*-fourth of the day; and *<u>for another fourth they confessed</u>* and worshiped the Lord their God.
> **Nehemiah 9:2-3**

This is a really interesting thing. It's very important to confess our sins and our forefathers' sins. The Israelites wanted to make sure they got all the sins taken care of, so they confessed sins for one fourth of the day. Dishonoring parents and using the Lord's Name in vain are common sins that I have everyone confess. These personal sins and the sins of our forefathers could be the cause of problems in our life. So I have people say, "In the Name of Jesus I confess the sins of my forefathers and my personal sins. And Lord, I ask You to forgive me, and I forgive my forefathers' sins.

CURSES

> 'The Lord is longsuffering and abundant in mercy, forgiving iniquity and transgression; but He by no means

clears the guilty, <u>visiting the iniquity of the fathers on the children to the third and fourth generation</u>.'

Numbers 14:18

Nationality Curses - Nationality curses are the stereotypes of your ancestors. What do you think of when you think of an Irishman? Beer, red hair, temper, fighting, etc. What do you think of when you think of an American Indian? Witchcraft, superstition, idolatry; and some of the tribes were very violent. Those are the stereotypes of your ancestors' nationalities. What nationalities are in your bloodlines? If you know the nationalities in your bloodlines, then you can name them and break the curses that come with them. Otherwise I say, "We break the curses of all the nationalities in my bloodline, known or unknown."

Ancestral Curses –

Characteristic Traits - Your family heritage is the characteristic traits in your family that repeat generation after generation. Whenever someone thinks of your family heritage, what do they think of? You know a lot of times they'll say, "Oh, they are all just mean," or "they're all stubborn". They may say, "they all fight, they'll fight at the drop of a hat", or "they're all alcoholics." Or they may say, "They are all just as sweet as can be". What is it they think about when they think about your family? Whatever your family heritage is; it could be a curse if it's a bad thing.

Sicknesses and Diseases – What type of sicknesses run through your family - cancer, diabetes, blood problems, heart problems, emphysema, etc? Those diseases that just seem to go right down your bloodline. With Americans of African descent, sickle cell disease and hypertension seem to be more predominant in the black culture than others, so those things are a curse. You don't have to suffer with those because basically there's no difference between you and I right now; we are one in Christ and we have a new Father with a new divine nature, so we can break the curses from that old bloodline.

Divorce – There is a lot of divorce in families. Today, when someone gets divorced, the whole family still accepts and loves them, and it's not such a bad thing. It used to be that people didn't get divorced because it was a bad thing. Well it doesn't seem to be a bad thing anymore because more than 50% of marriages end in divorce (even in the church). It all has to do with desensitization; people begin to think that since my grandparents were divorced and my parents divorced, it is okay for me to divorce. The curse just continues to repeat itself.

Bastard Curse –

> A bastard <u>shall not enter into</u> the congregation of the Lord; even to his <u>tenth generation</u> shall he not enter into the congregation of the Lord. Deuteronomy 23:2 (KJV)

A bastard curse runs for ten generations and will prevent one from entering into a close personal relationship with the Lord. Most people do not even know who their forefathers were four generations back, let alone ten generations back! If we do not know who they were, then we do not know their habits and behaviors. Therefore, I break the bastard curse with everyone I pray with.

SPOKEN CURSES -

> <u>Death and life are in the power of the tongue</u>, and those who love it will eat its fruit. Proverbs 18:21

> The hypocrite <u>with his mouth destroys his neighbor</u>, but through knowledge the righteous will be delivered.
> Proverbs 11:9

> Let <u>no corrupt word proceed out of your mouth</u>, but what is good for necessary edification, that it may impart grace to the hearers. Ephesians 4:29

There are witches, warlocks and other members of the occult that speak curses over people. Those words must be broken because they **can** have an effect upon a person's life. But the more common problem is the unkind and cruel words that were spoken over us as we were growing up. Those words were actually curses that have a **tremendous** effect on us because they were spoken by a person of authority in our life, someone who was supposed to love and protect us. Words like: "You idiot, can't you do anything right", "You are dumb", "You will never amount to anything", "You are not good for anything", and other damning phrases. The problem arises **after hearing it for a time, we begin to believe them, and agree with them, and then a stronghold is established.** To break out of these mindsets, we must use divine powered weapons of warfare.

> **For though we walk in the flesh, we do not war according to the flesh. ⁴For the weapons of our warfare *are* not carnal but mighty in God for pulling down strongholds, ⁵casting down arguments and every high thing that exalts itself against the knowledge of God, bringing every thought into captivity to the obedience of Christ, ...**
>
> **2 Corinthians 10:3-5**

To break these curses from your life, you need to confess your forefathers' and your own sins. Then, **IN THE NAME OF JESUS**, break the curses, bind all demons sent on assignment against you, cancel their assignments, and command them to leave you and your loved ones.

Then The Curses Become Undeserved Curses And Cannot Stay Upon You.

Like a fluttering sparrow or a darting swallow, <u>an undeserved curse does not come to rest</u>.
Proverbs 26:2 (NIV)

Like a flitting sparrow, like a flying swallow, so <u>a curse without cause shall not alight</u>. **Proverbs 26:2**

A word of caution: once a child gets out of your home and living on his own and begins to make wrong choices, he can bring these problems back upon himself. You can stop it for now, but your children have a free will to go back into sin and therefore invoke the curse again. They need to be trained in the way they should go in order to make the correct decisions in life.

Train up a child in the way he should go, and when he is old he will not depart from it. **Proverbs 22:6**

FALSE RELIGIONS:

I have everyone renounce, and break all ties with all false religions with which they have been involved. I classify a false religion as anything that is not preaching the fullness of the Godhead or deity of Jesus. I have everyone renounce all false teachings from other religions such as Eastern religions or secret societies. I also include all false teachings that do not line up with the Word of God in denominational, non-denominational, charismatic, Word of Faith, and the Catholic Church if they have been involved in any of them.

JUDGMENTS:

The Bible talks about how we make judgments on others and they come back to haunt us. Mom and Dad are usually judged the most because they are the ones who are making us deny our selfish nature and do the right thing. We may also judge other authority figures, such as babysitters, teachers, principals, pastors, or police. When we judge others, it will come back to us, sometimes quickly – sometimes later - but it will come back. The word of God is true and God is not a liar.

> **"Judge not, that you be not judged. 2For with what judgment you judge, you will be judged; and with the measure you use, it will be measured back to you.**
>
> **Matthew 7:1-2**

VOWS:

When we make judgments, we are critically judging someone for their behavior. The problem arises when we also make vows concerning our own future behavior. Some common vows we make are: I will never be like that; I will never do that; I will never marry someone like that; my kids will never do that; I will never treat my kids like that; I will never allow that to happen to me or my family; etc.

> "Again you have heard that it was said to those of old, 'You shall not swear falsely, but shall perform your oaths to the Lord.' ³⁴But I say to you, <u>do not swear at all</u>: neither by heaven, for it is God's throne; ³⁵nor by the earth, for it is His footstool; nor by Jerusalem, for it is the city of the great King. ³⁶Nor shall you swear by your head, because you cannot make one hair white or black. ³⁷But <u>let your 'Yes' be 'Yes,' and your 'No,' 'No</u>.' For whatever is more than these is from the evil one.
>
> **Matthew 5:33-37**

"LORD WILLING"

The problem is that you take control, and "**What Goes Around, Comes Around**". What we should be saying is found in the book of James.

> **Come now, you who say, "Today or tomorrow we will go to such and such a city, spend a year there, buy and sell, and make a profit"; 14whereas you do not know what *will happen* tomorrow. For what *is* your life? It is even a vapor that appears for a little time and then vanishes away. 15Instead you *ought* to say, "If the Lord wills, we shall live and do this or that."   James 4:13-15**

> **You are <u>snared</u> by the words of your mouth; you are taken by the words of your mouth.   Proverbs 6:2**

To Escape From The Snare You Have Caused.

When we make judgments and vows concerning how we, or a member of our family, will behave, we can entrap ourselves and other members of our family in wrong behaviors. Many times when I have led someone in prayers of repentance and to break judgments and vows, they have come back and told me how another member of their family has changed. It is amazing! I have everyone ask God to forgive them for making the judgments, then break the judgments they have made against all others, then renounce the vows they made about how they or a member of their family will not do certain things. Then I have them release everyone they have made judgments on thereby releasing themselves and their spouse and children. Then I have them pray God's will be done in their life and their families.

DEATH WISHES:

Many times when a person is going through some terrible abuse, they will give up and **"wish they were dead"**. That is speaking a **"death wish"** upon yourself. Sometimes they speak a death wish upon their tormentors; and then other times someone else may speak a death wish upon them. I have everyone break all **"death wishes"** they have spoken upon themselves, or upon others; and what others have spoken over them.

NOTES: TREATMENT MODALITIES

37 James Strong, Strong's Exhaustive Concordance: Compact Edition (Grand Rapids: Baker Book House, 1982), 128

38 Joseph H. Thayer, Thayer's Greek-English Lexicon of the New Testament, 4th ed. (Grand Rapids: Baker Book House, 1977), 131.

39 (James Strong), 613.

40 (Joseph H. Thayer), 385.

41 Spiros Zodhiates, The Hebrew/Greek Key Study Bible (World Publishers, 1991), 1204 (footnote).

EMOTIONAL INNER HEALING

◊ —— ◊

These are the areas I minister after deliverance. We must take care of the emotional hurts to protect against the demons coming back to the open wounds. It would be like putting a bandage on a wound without any healing balm. It will not heal properly, only continue to infect and fester.

BACKWARD SPIRIT

If someone experienced trauma before or during their birth, I will pray and ask Holy Spirit to turn their spirit around and let them know they are loved and needed as I minister scriptures to them. Let me explain. Pre-natal doctors will tell an expectant mother and father to talk or sing to their baby during the pregnancy in order to bond with the baby. The baby becomes familiar with the parents' voices and feels the love they extend. While the baby is in the womb, everything is supplied for his existence and he is content. My

Multiple Personality Disorder, Psychological or Demonic?

wife always said that the baby is in a floating water-bed with nothing to do but float around.

But, if his mother is going through strife and turmoil in her marriage or does not want the baby, it may be a totally different story. The baby senses all the turmoil and rejection on the outside, but is comfortable inside. And then all of a sudden, something begins to pull him outside where all the trouble is. He is afraid and does not want to leave his security; in his spirit and mind he turns around and says, "No, I don't want to go". Thus, he is born with a backward spirit. This can cause the person to be dyslexic, a slow learner in school, autistic, loners who never seemed to fit in with people, etc. We have ministered to people who were suffering from this, and it has changed their lives dramatically.

I will cite a few cases in particular. I was ministering to a group of people in Liberty, Texas and heard a young boy (ten years old) crying. I went to him and his mother and asked the mother what her marriage was like while she was pregnant with him. She said it was bad, and she divorced shortly after he was born. I laid my hand on his head and asked Holy Spirit to turn his backward spirit around as I ministered Psalm 39 and other scriptures. I asked Holy Spirit to let him know that he was not an accident or mistake, but that he was loved and needed and we could not do without him. He stopped crying, and then his mother told me he had dyslexia and was in special education doing second grade material. He should have been in the fifth grade. She said he could not read, so I opened my Bible and told him to read it. He began reading and never stumbled at all. I told his mom that it sounded good to me. He had three weeks left in school that year. **In three weeks time**, he went from second grade material to doing fifth grade and even eighth grade material in some of his classes. His teacher said he was an exemplary student, and he went back to regular classes the next year! Praise God! He wasn't dumb or retarded; he just suffered from a backward spirit because of the turmoil and rejection on the outside of the womb before he was born.

One mother came to me because her child's teacher had recommended she bring her son R_____ to me. R_____ was three years old and suffered from autism. His doctors had said that he would be in special education forever and there was no cure for his ailment. He had never spoken in a full sentence; usually he screamed and pointed at what he wanted. He would fixate on objects, was very selfish, would not share toys, and was not tolerant of others. His parents had taught him to respond with a mechanical hug when he was hugged. Otherwise, he showed no affection. This was R_____'s case history: his parents met and married in college. After graduation, mom had her career started and was doing great. Then she became pregnant and her "career" was ruined by the baby. She resented R_____ and never wanted him. He suffered tremendous rejection in the womb. I explained to them that the rejection was the cause of R_____'s sickness and that they needed to repent and be delivered from their own demons first. They agreed, and so

I ministered deliverance to mom and then dad. Then I had them bring R_____ to my office. I could not really pray for R_____ because he would not stand still, he was exploring everything in my office. Finally I had dad sit in a chair with mom sitting on the floor between his legs and R_____ sitting in her lap. I told her to hold him and I began to coach dad and mom how to minister to their son. I had them repent to R_____ and ask forgiveness of him for the rejection. Then I had them tell him that they loved him, wanted him, needed him, and was glad to have him as a son. Then we ministered scriptures, prayed, and asked God to turn R_____'s backward spirit around.

For someone who is suffering from this, I pray and ask God to turn their backward spirit around and let them know they are not an accident or a mistake and they are loved and needed. We cannot do without them! The scriptures we pray (in a paraphrase) are these:

For You formed my inward parts; You covered me in my mother's womb. 14I will praise You, for I am fearfully *and* wonderfully made; marvelous are Your works, and *that* my soul knows very well. 15My frame was not hidden from You, when I was made in secret, *and* skillfully wrought in the lowest parts of the earth. 16Your eyes saw my substance, being yet unformed. And in Your

book they all were written, the days fashioned for me, when *as yet there were* none of them.

Psalm 139:13-16

For as the body is one and has many members, but all the members of that one body, being many, are one body, so also *is* Christ. ¹³For by one Spirit we were all baptized into one body—whether Jews or Greeks, whether slaves or free—and have all been made to drink into one Spirit. ¹⁴For in fact the body is not one member but many. ¹⁵If the foot should say, "Because I am not a hand, I am not of the body," is it therefore not of the body? ¹⁶And if the ear should say, "Because I am not an eye, I am not of the body," is it therefore not of the body? ¹⁷If the whole body *were* an eye, where *would be* the hearing? If the whole *were* hearing, where *would be* the smelling? <u>¹⁸But now God has set the members, each one of them, in the body just as He pleased</u>. ¹⁹And if they *were* all one member, where *would* the body *be*? ²⁰But now indeed *there are* many members, yet one body. ²¹And the eye cannot say to the hand, "I have no need of you"; nor again the head to the feet, "I have no need of you." ²²No, much rather, <u>those members of the body which seem to be weaker are necessary</u>. <u>²³And those *members* of the body which we think to be less honorable, on these we bestow greater</u>

honor; and our unpresentable *parts* have greater modesty, 24but our presentable *parts* have no need. **But God composed the body, having given greater honor to that *part* which lacks it,** 25that there should be no schism in the body, but *that* the members should have the same care for one another. 26And if one member suffers, all the members suffer with *it;* or if one member is honored, all the members rejoice with *it.* 27Now you are the body of Christ, and members individually.

1 Corinthians 12:12-27

For we are His workmanship, created in Christ Jesus for good works, which God prepared beforehand that we should walk in them.

Ephesians 2:10

That night we did not see any change, so we ministered to R_____'s parents that they are not to go by what they see, but to receive by faith what God had done in R_____ that night. We do not live by sight, but by faith.

For we walk by faith, not by sight.

2 Corinthians 5:7

Multiple Personality Disorder, Psychological or Demonic?

That was on a Friday night, and Sunday they went to church as usual. Mom dropped R_____ off in the nursery and, as was the custom, Grandma would pick him up when the service was over. Normally, R_____ would not share toys and would be sitting by himself or fixated on the drinking fountain or something similar. That day when Grandma arrived at the nursery, R_____ was sitting in the middle of the floor playing with the other children and sharing toys. When he saw Grandma, he got up, ran to her, yelled out "That's my Grandma", and gave her a big hug and kiss. Remember, R_____ did not talk or show affection. It almost gave Grandma a heart attack. It took just three days for R_____'s healing and deliverance of a backward spirit from rejection in the womb to manifest. It was glorious! He was in the grave on Friday, but set free on Sunday morning! Hallelujah! The world says there is no cure for autism, but **nothing is impossible with God!** A few months later, I received a call from R_____'s dad. He was crying and thanking me for giving him the son he always dreamed of having. His dream was to take his son to a major league baseball game, but R_____ could not sit still that long before. That day he was on his way home after spending the afternoon at an Astros game with R_____! Thank you, Jesus! I thank God for allowing me to be His instrument for healing. I take no glory for what **He has done**.

FRAGMENTED SOUL:

A person suffers from a fragmented soul when there is emotional turmoil because of ungodly soul ties with others. The ties pull at our emotions from different directions, and we are tormented from within. I pray for the Lord Jesus to restore a person's soul as He promised He would do in the Word.

> **He restores my soul; He leads me in the paths of righteousness for His name's sake.   Psalm 23:3**

> **He has redeemed my soul in peace from the battle *that was* against me, for there were many against me.**
> **Psalm 55:18**

SPIRIT WOUNDS:

People can be very harsh at times. Sometimes words are spoken against us that really hurt us and cut us deep. When I was growing up, there was a saying we would repeat when others would say ugly things to us. "Sticks and stones may break my bones, but words will never hurt me". I realize now that was a lie from Satan; because we retain those words, and if not dealt with, they can torment us and cause turmoil and pain later in life.

The words of a talebearer *are* like tasty trifles, and they go down into the inmost body.   **Proverbs 18:8**

A person's inmost being is their spirit-man, and it can be wounded by the words that cut us deep within.

The spirit of a man will sustain him in sickness, but who can bear a broken spirit?   **Proverbs 18:14**

When praying for this, I will ask God to pour the healing balm of Gilead on the spirit wounds, heal the hurts, and wash away the scars of the words that have wounded their spirit.

BROKEN HEART:

People can suffer from a broken heart as a result of trauma and other events of life. God anointed Jesus, and He gave us that same anointing to heal the brokenhearted. So we lay our hand on the person's heart, thank God for the anointing, and command the broken heart to be healed. We ask God to bind it with cords of love that cannot be broken. We will ask Holy Spirit to take them back in their memories to the point of origin of the hurts and speak peace and healing to them, dispelling any lies they have believed as a result of the trauma. When Jesus heals their heart, they still have the memory, but the sting is gone.

> **The LORD *is* near to those who have a broken heart, and saves such as have a contrite spirit.**   **Psalm 34:18**

> **"The Spirit of the Lord GOD *is* upon Me, because the LORD has anointed Me To preach good tidings to the poor; He has sent Me to heal the brokenhearted, To proclaim liberty to the captives, and the opening of the prison to *those who are* bound; ²to proclaim the acceptable year of the LORD, and the day of vengeance of our God; to comfort all who mourn,**   **Isaiah 61:1-2**

> **"The Spirit of the LORD is upon Me, Because He has anointed Me To preach the gospel to the poor; <u>He has sent Me to heal the brokenhearted</u>, To proclaim liberty to the captives And recovery of sight to the blind, To set at liberty those who are oppressed;**   **Luke 4:18**

AFFIRMATION:

One of the biggest problems I see in the world today is the lack of love shown by fathers to their children. If there was a bad relationship with father, it will usually be transferred to the relationship with God. If dad denied affection and approval, they will not trust God to provide what He has already given. So, after ministering deliverance, I will talk to a person as their father. I will apologize to them and tell them I was the one who was wrong, not them. I was the one who had the problems. I will apologize for the things I said and did to them that were wrong. I tell them I love them and am proud of them. I apologize for not saying those things when they were growing up. I accept them as my child and tell them I am glad we had you. I tell them I know it is hard to do and I do not deserve it, but would they please forgive me.

It is amazing what happens when I minister this. I was in Costa Rica ministering in a church of about 800 people. My translator was on the platform with a wired microphone and I had a wireless mic, so I was walking around as I was talking to the people as their father. Suddenly I realized the translator was not talking. I turned and looked at him; he was lying on the stage, curled up in a fetus position, and was crying. I continued to minister, and God was healing even though I was not speaking Spanish! There were some people in that church calling me papa when I left.

I ministered deliverance and emotional healing to a pastor and his wife from Croatia. They were at least twenty years older than me, but afterwards I would receive letters from his wife, and she would write them to "Papa" Morris. I pray that parents would realize the power of the words they speak over their children. They are life or death to them. God wants to turn the hearts of children to their fathers, so they will also turn to Him and receive all the blessings of a child of God.

Death and life are in the power of the tongue, and those who love it will eat its fruit. **Proverbs 18:21**

And he will turn the <u>hearts of the fathers to the children</u>, and the <u>hearts of the children to their fathers</u>, lest I come and strike the earth with a curse." **Malachi 4:6**

He will also go before Him in the spirit and power of Elijah, <u>'to turn the hearts of the fathers to the children,'</u> and the disobedient to the wisdom of the just, to make ready a people prepared for the Lord." **Luke 1:17**

ADOPTION:

A lot of people do not feel like they belong, or that they are part of a family. They suffer from rejection and loneliness. I pray and loose the spirit of adoption upon them.

> **For you did not receive the spirit of bondage again to fear, but you received the Spirit of adoption by whom we cry out, "Abba, Father."**
> **Romans 8:15**

I tell them that they have a "Daddy God" who loves them and will always have time for them. He will never leave them or forsake them, will always listen to their prayers, and He wants to bless them. After this prayer, people have said that they feel loved and wanted;

and that they finally have a sense of belonging and being a part of the family of God.

SPIRIT OF POWER, LOVE, & SOUND MIND:

For God has not given us a spirit of fear, but of power and of love and of a sound mind.
2 Timothy 1:7

God has given us the spirit of power, love and a sound mind, but the events we suffer growing up diminish those, so I ask God to restore these in the person.

CLOSING PRAYER

After ministering, I will lay my hand on their head and close all the doors that demons were behind and seal them with the blood of Jesus. Then I ask Holy Spirit to carry unto completion the good work he began in them:

being confident of this very thing, that He who has begun a good work in you will complete *it* until the day of Jesus Christ;
Philippians 1:6

GOD'S WILL FOR US IS AN ABUNDANT LIFE

Jesus has purchased a wonderful life for us because he loves us so much. He willingly gave up his blessed life in heaven and came to earth; He died willingly for us so we would not have to live in torment.

The thief does not come except to steal, and to kill, and to destroy. <u>I (Jesus) have come that they may have life, and that they may have _it_ more abundantly</u>.   John 10:10

CONCLUSION

In all this writing, I am not saying that helping a person with Multiple Personality Disorder is not a complicated ordeal. **On the contrary, it is complicated**. It is not the same as working with a person who is suffering with dependency issues or other emotional traumas. In working with MPD, one must develop a deeper therapeutic alliance with the client, while depending on the power of Holy Spirit to deliver them from the oppression. In my empirical opinion, this is a spiritual issue that must be addressed on a spiritual level. In order to do that, one must first have a personal relationship with Jesus Christ as Lord of their life. A born again Christian **cannot** be demon possessed, but the personality nests that are formed do hinder them living the abundant life that Jesus purchased for them. Jesus and Holy Spirit have given us the authority and power to defeat the enemy of our souls, and I believe this is His prescription for victory over Multiple Personality Disorder.

We do not go through life just bumping around from accident to accident. God has a plan for all our lives. You all are on a divine appointment as you read this book, and I am excited. God bless you as you receive your healing and deliverance.

Jesus and I love you,
Phillip Morris, Ph.D.

BIBLIOGRAPHY

Dickason, C. Fred, Demon Possession and the Christian: A New Perspective, Chicago: Moody Press, 1987

Friesen, James G., More than Survivors: Conversations with Multiple-Personality Clients, San Bernardino: Here's Life Publishers, 1992

Friesen, James G. Uncovering the Mystery of MPD: Its Shocking Origins ... its Surprising Cure, San Bernardino: Here's Life Publishers, 1991

Hammond, Frank, Pigs in the Parlor: A Practical Guide to Deliverance, Kirkwood: Impact Books, Inc., 1973

Kaplan, Harold I., and Benjamin J. Sadock, Synopsis of Psychiatry: Behavioral Sciences, Clinical Psychiatry, 5th ed., Edited by

Robert Cancro and Jack A. Grebb, Baltimore: Williams & Wilkins, 1988

Morris, Phillip S., Spiritual Connections to Personality Disorders, Columbus: Brentwood Christian Press, 1991

Strong, James, Strong's Exhaustive Concordance: Compact Edition, Reprint, Grand Rapids: Baker Book House, 1982

Thayer, Joseph H., Thayer's Greek-English Lexicon of the New Testament, 4th ed, Grand Rapids: Baker Book House, 1977

The American College Dictionary, Edited by C.L. Barnhart and Jess Stein, New York: Random House, 1967

The American Psychiatric Association: Diagnostic and Statistical Manual of Mental Disorders, Third Edition, Revised, Washington DC: American Psychiatric Association, 1987

Unger, Merrill F., Demons in the World Today: A Study of Occultism in Light of God's Word, Wheaton: Tyndale House Publishers, 1988

Unger, Merrill F., What Demons Can Do to Saints, Chicago: Moody Press, 1991

Vine, W.E., Vine's Expository Dictionary of Old and New Testament Words, Old Testament Edited by F.F. Bruce, New Jersey: Fleming H. Revell Company, 1981

Zodhiates, Spiros, The Hebrew/Greek Key Study Bible, World Publishers, 1991

About The Author

D r. Morris was born and raised in Indiana and then came to Houston in 1979 to attend Gulf Coast Bible College. He graduated from Christian College of America with a degree in Psychology/Counseling, and a Master of Arts in Pastoral Counseling from Houston Graduate School of Theology. He earned his Doctor of Philosophy in Theology from Christian Bible College and Seminary.

In 1982, God thrust Phillip into the deliverance ministry and called him to "establish the church" by "setting the captives free". Pastor Phillip founded Restoration House Church in 1992, and also has a residential treatment program through Restore to More Ministries. His previous books include "Spiritual Connections to Personality Disorders", "Body Piercing", "Walking Out Your Deliverance", and other booklets.

Dr. Morris travels to teach and minister spiritual warfare and deliverance locally, nationally, and internationally. To schedule speaking engagements or deliverance appointments, you may contact him at Restoration Church, 1609 Jones Road, Highlands, TX 77562 or www.restorationhousechurch.com.

Dr. Phillip Morris is married, has four children and numerous wonderful grandchildren and a great-grandson. Phillip served two tours in Vietnam, was dead on arrival after a car accident in 1970, and then finally accepted Jesus Christ as his Lord and Savior in 1976.

CPSIA information can be obtained
at www.ICGtesting.com
Printed in the USA
LVOW11s0755020317
525917LV00001B/100/P

9 781606 477328